Social Issues in Literature

Family Dysfunction in William Faulkner's *As I Lay Dying*

Other Books in the Social Issues in Literature Series:

Colonialism in Joseph Conrad's *Heart of Darkness*
Death and Dying in the Poetry of Emily Dickinson
Democracy in the Poetry of Walt Whitman
Depression in Sylvia Plath's *The Bell Jar*
The Environment in Rachel Carson's *Silent Spring*
The Food Industry in Eric Schlosser's *Fast Food Nation*
Poverty in John Steinbeck's *The Pearl*
Race in John Howard Griffin's *Black Like Me*
Race in William Shakespeare's *Othello*
Slavery in Toni Morrison's *Beloved*
Teen Issues in S.E. Hinton's *The Outsiders*
Women's Issues in Zora Neale Hurston's *Their Eyes Were Watching God*

Social Issues in Literature

Family Dysfunction in William Faulkner's *As I Lay Dying*

Claudia Durst Johnson, Book Editor

GREENHAVEN PRESS
A part of Gale, Cengage Learning

Detroit • New York • San Francisco • New Haven, Conn • Waterville, Maine • London

Elizabeth Des Chenes, *Director, Publishing Solutions*

© 2013 Greenhaven Press, a part of Gale, Cengage Learning

Gale and Greenhaven Press are registered trademarks used herein under license.

For more information, contact:
Greenhaven Press
27500 Drake Rd.
Farmington Hills, MI 48331-3535
Or you can visit our Internet site at gale.cengage.com

ALL RIGHTS RESERVED.
No part of this work covered by the copyright herein may be reproduced, transmitted, stored, or used in any form or by any means graphic, electronic, or mechanical, including but not limited to photocopying, recording, scanning, digitizing, taping, Web distribution, information networks, or information storage and retrieval systems, except as permitted under Section 107 or 108 of the 1976 United States Copyright Act, without the prior written permission of the publisher.

For product information and technology assistance, contact us at

Gale Customer Support, 1-800-877-4253
For permission to use material from this text or product, submit all requests online at www.cengage.com/permissions

Further permissions questions can be emailed to permissionrequest@cengage.com

Articles in Greenhaven Press anthologies are often edited for length to meet page requirements. In addition, original titles of these works are changed to clearly present the main thesis and to explicitly indicate the author's opinion. Every effort is made to ensure that Greenhaven Press accurately reflects the original intent of the authors. Every effort has been made to trace the owners of copyrighted material.

Cover image © Everett Collection Inc./Alamy.

LIBRARY OF CONGRESS CATALOGING-IN-PUBLICATION DATA

Family dysfunction in William Faulkner's As I lay dying / Claudia Durst Johnson, book editor.
    p. cm. -- (Social issues in literature)
Includes bibliographical references and index.
ISBN 978-0-7377-6385-0 (hardcover)
ISBN 978-0-7377-6386-7 (pbk.)
1. Faulkner, William, 1897-1962. As I lay dying. 2. Dysfunctional families in literature. I. Johnson, Claudia Durst, 1938-
PS3511.A86A865 2013
813'.52--dc23

2012042116

Printed in the USA
   2 3 4 5 6   30 29 28 27 26

Contents

Introduction	9
Chronology	12

Chapter 1: Background on William Faulkner

1. Faulkner's Growth as a Writer   16
   Linda Wagner-Martin

   William Faulkner, who resisted formal education and wrote in a modern, experimental stream-of-consciousness style, became a giant in the literary world and won the Nobel Prize for Literature.

2. Faulkner's Economic Struggles   26
   Joseph Blotner

   Although Faulkner gained much fame as author of *The Sound and the Fury* and *As I Lay Dying* the income he received for his work was not sufficient to live on, and he struggled financially.

3. Faulkner's Dysfunctional Family   33
   Judith Bryant Wittenberg

   Faulkner's own family is reflected in the mother, father, and siblings of the Bundren family.

Chapter 2: *As I Lay Dying* and Family Dysfunction

1. Faulkner's View of the Bundren Family   42
   William Faulkner

   Addie's release from marriage and family in death brings conflict and disorder to the fore.

2. Faulkner's Characters in an Insane World   49
   William Rossky

   The insane chaos of the real world is mirrored in the egotism and blindness of a damaged family.

3. Family Conflict and Verbal Fictions 55
   in *As I Lay Dying*
   John Earl Bassett

   Maternal cruelty leads to disruption and revenge.

4. The Culture of Religious Suppression 62
   in *As I Lay Dying*
   Nanci Kincaid

   The Bundren family, especially Addie and Dewey Dell, are destroyed by a religion that sees living itself as evil.

5. Maternal Influence in *As I Lay Dying* 71
   Marc Hewson

   Addie is an active force in the lives of her children, an example of emotion and human involvement, as opposed to the male inaction and cold egotism of her husband.

6. Feminine and Maternal Rebellion 81
   in *As I Lay Dying*
   Amy Louise Wood

   Addie and Dewey Dell both react negatively to motherhood.

7. Father as Victim as Well as Villain 88
   Rita Rippetoe

   Although Anse is usually regarded as the egoist villain of the novel, he is also a victim of poverty and mental disorder.

8. Jewel as Outsider and Man of Action 95
   Peter G. Beidler

   Jewel, Addie's illegitimate son, is an illustration of the family's dysfunction in his decision to separate himself from his siblings and in his hot-tempered attacks on them.

9. Vardaman's Reactions to Death Are Normal 101
   Floyd C. Watkins and William Dillingham

   Vardaman should be interpreted as a normal child, traumatized by his mother's death. He is not an idiot.

Chapter 3: Contemporary Perspectives on Family Dysfunction

1. Child Neglect Is Prevalent but Not Widely Understood   107
   Cailin O'Connor and Maggie McKenna

   Emotional neglect of children is often caused by parental depression, social isolation, and stress.

2. Marriage May Not Be Essential for a Functional Family   112
   Jessica Bennett and Jesse Ellison

   Many of the practical reasons for marriage no longer apply, so love has become more important, and such relationships can still create well-functioning families.

3. Some Women Have No Instinct for Mothering   117
   Mary Sojourner

   Some women love their children but hate being mothers, a condition that may be attributable to brain cells.

4. Fathers Are Important in the Healthy Development of Children   123
   Jeffrey Rosenberg and W. Bradford Wilcox

   Involved fathers are key to healthy and emotionally stable children.

5. Mom's Favoritism Can Affect Kids, Sibling Rivalry as Adults   129
   Sharon Jayson

   Maternal favoritism, while very common, impacts self-esteem and can have long-lasting effects into adulthood.

For Further Discussion	136
For Further Reading	137
Bibliography	138
Index	143

Introduction

On June 4, 2012, the *New York Times* ran an article by Frank Bruni titled "The Enigma Beside Edwards," about a very public dysfunctional family—that of former North Carolina governor and presidential candidate John Edwards, who was on trial for misuse of campaign funds to support and hide his mistress and their illegitimate child. Edwards's wife, Elizabeth, had been diagnosed with terminal cancer well before Edwards's affair began, and her discovery of his betrayal, as well as her realization that her husband had, by the affair, destroyed his chances for the presidency, had resulted in at least one humiliating public outburst of rage. It was not the first trauma for the family, whose sixteen-year-old son had died in a car accident in 1996. Edwards's daughter Cate, a lawyer like her mother and father, endured the death of her mother and then the trial of her philandering father, standing by him each day of his trial to hear excruciating stories of the effect his behavior had on her mother.

Some of the oldest stories in civilization hinge on family dysfunction: Agamemnon sacrificing his daughter to win a battle, Oedipus unwittingly murdering his father and marrying his mother, Cain murdering his brother Abel, to name a few. We are reminded by these stories and stories like that of John Edwards that domestic conflict is as persistent throughout history as the family unit itself.

Dysfunctionalism is created by many elements, among them loveless marriages, forced marriages, parental insensitivity, emotional neglect of children, poverty, physical and/or emotional abuse, parental favoritism, harmful traditions and conventions, addiction, and unrealistic expectations. The results are sibling rivalry, struggles for attention, loneliness and feelings of abandonment, resentment, feelings of inadequacy, self-importance, delusions, and warped views of marriage and the family. William Faulkner's *As I Lay Dying* is a literary reminder produced in the twentieth century of a situation that is as persistent as rain and as damaging as a flood.

Faulkner's novel's importance is seen in an analysis by E.L. Doctorow that appeared in the *New York Review of Books* on May 24, 2012. The degeneration of individual members of the family is outlined here: Addie's physical and psychological exhaustion and bitterness, Anse's manipulation and greed, Dewey Dell's attempt to have an abortion only to have her father take her money for a new set of teeth, Darl's seeming madness in burning down the barn where his mother's corpse lies, Jewel's coldness and repudiation of the family in favor of his horse, Vardaman's confusion in speaking of his mother as a fish, and Cash's heroics in saving his mother's coffin for which he is paid with concrete being poured on his bare leg in place of a medically applied cast.

Although the novel takes place in rural Mississippi, there is little mention of a larger context except for Darl's serving in World War I. Poverty and race are not raised as social issues in the novel, but the background is worth a brief mention. The paths poor whites in the South were forced to follow into poverty were varied. In the 1920s many of the families of the poor had been in poverty since before the Civil War, when they worked for large landowners. But the forebears of some of the poor had once been large landowners themselves, lost everything they had after the Civil War, and became small landowners or tenant farmers on land owned by others. There was a slight resurgence in the fortune of farmers immediately after World War I, but by the mid-1920s, war-ravaged Europe had rallied, land and produce prices in the South plummeted, and farmers were already experiencing the economic depression that would not hit the rest of the country until the 1930s.

It is difficult to be exact about the socioeconomic history of the Bundren ancestry. Addie's position as a schoolteacher is strong evidence that her family was sufficiently well placed to provide her with more than the usual eighth-grade education, and they owned a respectable plot in the Jefferson cemetery. Anse owned land at the time of their marriage, still had land at the time of the novel, and may even have had the money to pay for migrant labor (like Lafe), but the Bundrens, whether or not Anse actually has adequate money to provide them with a decent life, live in poverty. Dewey Dell, Addie's daughter, picks crops instead of teaching school.

Like the Bundrens, many families in today's economic climate have fallen into poverty and are experiencing the ensuing results. Contemporary signs of family dysfunction parallel those in Faulkner's novel: suppression of feelings, emotional neglect of children, emotionally detached parents, sibling rivalry, the institution of marriage, and motherhood. The contributors in this volume discuss how William Faulkner expresses and deals with these issues in his masterwork *As I Lay Dying*.

Chronology

September 25, 1897
William Faulkner is born in Mississippi.

1916
Faulkner tries his hand at art and poetry in Oxford, Mississippi.

July 9, 1918
After being turned down by the US Army, Faulkner enlists in the Canadian Royal Air Force.

December 1918
Faulkner is discharged from military service and returns to Oxford.

1921
Faulkner takes a job as postmaster at the University of Mississippi.

1924
Publishes *The Marble Faun*; his job as university postmaster comes to an end.

1925
Travels to New Orleans and tours Europe.

1926
Publishes *Soldiers' Pay*.

1927
Publishes *Mosquitoes*.

1929
Publishes *Sartoris* and *The Sound and the Fury*.

1930

Publishes *As I Lay Dying*.

1931

Publishes *Sanctuary*.

1932

Becomes a contract writer for MGM in California, the first of several such contracts with Hollywood studios; publishes *Light in August*.

1936

Publishes *Absalom, Absalom!*

1938

Publishes *The Unvanquished*.

1940

Publishes *The Hamlet*.

1942

Publishes *Go Down, Moses*.

1948

Publishes *Intruder in the Dust*.

1950

Receives the Nobel Prize in Literature; publishes *Requiem for a Nun*.

1951

Receives National Book Award for *Collected Stories*.

1954

Publishes *A Fable*.

1955
A Fable wins the National Book Award for Fiction, as well as the Pulitzer Prize.

1957
Begins long-standing residency at the University of Virginia and publishes *The Town*.

1960
Accepts a faculty position at the University of Virginia.

1962
On June 17 is injured from his third fall from a horse in five years and dies on July 7.

Social Issues in Literature

CHAPTER 1

Background on William Faulkner

Faulkner's Growth as a Writer

Linda Wagner-Martin

Linda Wagner-Martin is the Frank Borden Hanes Professor of English and Comparative Literature at the University of North Carolina–Chapel Hill. She is the author and editor of fifty volumes, including one on criticism of William Faulkner's works.

William Faulkner, a Mississippian born William Cuthbert Falkner in 1929, adhered to his vocation as a writer, sometimes living marginally from meager returns from the publication of his novels and short stories, and remaining most of his life in the small university town of Oxford, Mississippi. From humble literary beginnings, he achieved the status of one of the greatest modern fiction writers and was awarded the Nobel Prize for Literature. As I Lay Dying *has often been regarded as the greatest novel of his early period, appearing within a short time of his best-known work,* The Sound and the Fury. *The two novels were among his most puzzling to readers and critics alike, but they secured his reputation in the literary world. Although Faulkner himself was not happily married, he cherished the ideal of loving responsibility, which is so blatantly missing from* As I Lay Dying.

William Faulkner is considered by many readers to have been America's greatest modern writer. His fiction satisfies the critical demands that writing be inventive and invigorating, as ready to release the imagination as it is to channel it. Each of Faulkner's novels is a distinct structure of language, carefully shaped to achieve its own distinct meaning. Faulkner faces the problematic existence of the modern world, and he

---

Linda Wagner-Martin, "William Faulkner," *American Novelists, 1910–1945 (Part 1: Adamic-Fisher, Part 2: Fitzgerald-Rolvaag, Part 3: Sandoz-Young)*, James J. Martine. Detroit: Gale Research, 1981. Copyright © 1982 Cengage Learning. All rights reserved. Reproduced by permission.

insists that human beings can surmount those problems. As he said in his Nobel Prize address, "I believe that man will not merely endure: he will prevail. He is immortal, not because he alone among creatures has an inexhaustible voice, but because he has a soul, a spirit capable of compassion and sacrifice and endurance." Faulkner portrays in his fiction all the qualities he finds necessary for truly human and humane existence—honor, respect, love; bravery, loyalty, humor; responsibility, reverence, fear. . . .

Scorning Formal Education

Faulkner's childhood was filled with projects and games involving his three younger brothers (Murry, born in 1899; John, born in 1901; and Dean, born in 1907) and his cousin Sallie Murry Wilkins, who was the same age as Murry Faulkner. Estelle Oldham, his wife-to-be, was another close playmate. Faulkner was a good student in his younger elementary days, but by sixth grade he was playing hooky whenever he had the opportunity. In high school, he was more interested in playing football than in studying. He liked to write and draw, and he illustrated the stories and poems he had written. He seemed often to live in a world of imaginary characters and events, and was eager to miss social events if his parents would permit him to.

Faulkner stopped attending school midway through the eleventh and final grade at Oxford High School. He went back briefly in the fall of 1915 because he wanted to play football once again and, despite his slight stature (he was 5' 5" at the time and grew only another half inch), he made the first string (for the first time), as quarterback. Leaving high school for good once the season was over, he was put to work in early 1916 as a bookkeeper in his grandfather's bank. He had no interest in the job and did little work. His real interest was in reading the avant-garde literature to which he had been introduced by Phil Stone. A native of Oxford and four years older than Faulkner, Stone had cum laude bachelor's degrees from both the University of Mississippi and Yale. Returning to Oxford in the summer of 1914 to study law at the university, he and Faulkner soon became friends, and he was to contribute much to Faulkner's literary education, commenting on Faulkner's writing and introducing him to new books. He also introduced Faulkner to another Oxford native, the writer Stark Young, who, although he had left his job at the University of Mississippi to teach literature at the University of Texas, returned to Oxford each summer. Young proved to be another of Faulkner's early mentors. In the fall of 1916, after Stone had completed his law degree at the University of Mississippi and gone to Yale to pursue a second L.L.B. [law degree], Faulkner began to spend more time around the university campus, forming another important friendship with a freshman named Ben Wasson, who was later to serve as his literary agent. Although he was not a student at the university, drawings by Faulkner were included in the school's yearbooks for 1916–1917 and 1917–1918.

Still discontent with his job at the bank, where he was actually spending very little time, Faulkner had further cause for unhappiness in early 1918 when Estelle Oldham announced her engagement to Cornell Franklin. She and Faulkner had planned to marry, but both sets of parents forbade their union. Faulkner had no profession; Franklin was an established lawyer. Estelle Oldham offered to elope with Faulkner, but he wanted her father's consent so she drifted into a marriage that proved to be unhappy, and Faulkner vowed to enter the military as soon as possible. After being turned down for aviation training in the U. S. Army Signal Corps, he went to New Haven [Connecticut] to spend some time with Phil Stone. In July he enlisted in the Canadian division of the RAF [Royal Air Force], but World War I ended before he could complete his flight training. He remained fascinated with flying throughout his life, however; and he returned home from Canada wearing his RAF uniform and telling stories that suggested that he had had a glowing military career. . . .

Finances, Marriage, and Work

In January or February 1929, around the time Harrison Smith agreed to publish *The Sound and the Fury*, Faulkner set out to "invent the most horrific tale I could imagine . . ." with the conscious intention of making money. The tale was *Sanctuary*, the most violent and sensational of Faulkner's novels. One of the reasons for Faulkner's increased concern about money was that he was about to marry a divorced woman with two children. Estelle Oldham Franklin had separated from Cornell Franklin in 1927 and in April 1929 her divorce became final. The immediate prospects for Faulkner's money-making project were not good, however. The consensus about the manuscript at the offices of Cape & Smith, where Faulkner had sent it in the late spring of 1929, was that it was too shocking, unpublishable. In the introduction for the 1932 Modern Library edition of *Sanctuary*, Faulkner remembered Smith's writing, "Good God, I can't publish this. We'd both be in jail." Despite this setback Faulkner and Estelle Franklin were married on 20 June 1929. After spending the summer in Pascagoula, Mississippi, they returned to Oxford, where Faulkner took a job working nights at the university power plant. To the hum of the dynamo at the power plant, he wrote *As I Lay Dying* (1930), which would prove to be his next published novel.

Writing *As I Lay Dying*

Faulkner later said of the composition of this novel, "I set out deliberately to write a tour-de-force. Before I ever put pen to paper and set down the first word I knew what the last word would be and almost where the last period would fall. . . . That other quality which *The Sound and the Fury* had given me was absent: that emotion definite and physical and yet nebulous to describe: that ecstasy, that eager and joyous faith and anticipation of surprise which the yet unmarred sheet beneath my hand held inviolate and unfailing, waiting for release.... I said, More than likely I shall never again have to know this much [of] a book before I begin to write it...." Despite the difference in the methods of composition, *The Sound and the Fury* and *As I Lay Dying* have often been paired by critics who point to them as Faulkner's most brilliant stylistic experiments. The sheer audacity of Faulkner's employing structures and narrative methods that conflicted with all the conventions of fiction has to be considered; yet if these novels did not deal with themes that speak to every reader, few people would have bothered to learn to appreciate the craft. For readers in the late 1920s, accustomed to the accumulation of details and straightforward plots of a realistic writer such as Theodore Dreiser, Faulkner's stylistic innovations posed many problems. That Faulkner's experimentation was accepted by a contemporary audience is a tribute to the centrality of his theme: the need for balance between the demands of self and responsibility to one's society.

As I Lay Dying presents this responsibility as the family's obligation to fulfill their promise to Addie Bundren, their dying mother, who has asked to be buried with her kin. Although she is central to the novel, she speaks only one of the fifty-nine interior monologues into which the novel is divided. Mistrustful of language, of rhetoric, Addie has lived and dies through action. That she has Faulkner's sympathy is clear from the opposition he creates for her in her husband, Anse. One of the laziest characters in American fiction, Anse has a kind of bewildering charm (he believes that he will die if he ever sweats, a wonderful ruse for one who lives in Mississippi before the days of air conditioning); he believes that his children and friends are put on earth purposely to care for him (and he is ever a God-fearing man); but the real evil in his character becomes clear as the novel progresses, and we see what living with such a man—emotionally dead from the beginning—has done to Addie. As Dr. Peabody and the neighbors Tull and Samson give reliable perspectives, it soon becomes poignantly clear how little Addie has had in her life.

Another Family Novel

Another family novel [as was *The Sound and the Fury*], the book's principal characters are the parents and the five children. Again, one sister (Dewey Dell, pregnant with an illegitimate child) is set against her brothers. This time there are four: Cash, the builder who sacrifices self for his family; Darl, the clairvoyant and eventually insane child who wants his mother's love desperately; Jewel, the illegitimate son of the minister and his mother's favorite; and Vardaman, the youngest and the one most affected by his mother's death. Yet, unlike Caddy [in *The Sound and the Fury*], Dewey Dell is not at the center of her brothers' existence; the novel's focus is more often on the mother's relationship with the children and on the brothers' interactions with each other. A range of emotion colors the chronological presentation of Addie's death, funeral, and what should have been a simple journey to Jefferson (some forty miles away). Anger, hatred, jealousy, loyalty, reverence, fear—Faulkner creates a panorama as he presents the characters dramatically. In *As I Lay Dying* he took his structure from the play script; the name of the speaker appears above each segment of the story. In the interweaving of parts lies the fantastic artistry of the novel, not only accomplishing the narrative proper but also creating a subtle blend of tone so that *As I Lay Dying* has been called comic as often as it has been called tragic. That it is both, and that part of its impact comes from the shifting points of view of fifteen different speakers that blend, contrast, and finally illuminate, is to Faulkner's highest credit.

Faulkner sets up polarities between male and female as often as he does between the cultured and the peasant (*As I Lay*

Family Dysfunction in William Faulkner's As I Lay Dying

Author William Faulkner photographed in his Oxford, Mississippi, home in 1950. © Corbis.

Dying is usually considered different from *The Sound and the Fury* because its characters are common folk, a distinction that seems to have existed in critics' minds more regularly than in Faulkner's), between the old South and the new, and between the urban and the rural. Here, and in other Faulkner novels as well, the female is an active force—passionate, protective, and strong—as when Addie says with a deep irony, "I would be I; I would let him be the shape and echo of his word." For Anse and the Reverend Whitfield, rhetoric might suffice; for Addie, "words are no good. . . . I knew that motherhood was invented by someone who had to have a word for it because the ones that had the children didn't care whether there was a word for it or not. I knew that fear was invented by someone that had never had the fear; pride, who never had the pride. . . . I would think how words go straight up in a thin line quick and harmless, and how terribly doing goes along the earth, clinging to it, so that after a while the two lines are too far apart for the same person to straddle from one to the other. . . ." In his later fiction, Faulkner created male characters who are also chary of language and mistrustful of people (such as Gavin Stevens [protagonist of *Intruder in the Dust*]) who dissipate their feeling into fluency. In his early and middle fiction, these strong, silent characters were usually women.

Faulkner's Family Responsibilities

As I Lay Dying was published on 6 October 1930. Most of the reviews expressed qualified praise, but again, while they added to Faulkner's stature as a novelist, their praise was not translated into good sales. As soon as he had sent off *As I Lay Dying*, Faulkner had turned, as he would often during the 1930s, to writing short fiction that he hoped would interest the editors of popular magazines. As the 1930s wore on, he became increasingly successful at placing short fiction in such high-paying magazines as the *Saturday Evening Post*. During that same time, Faulkner's financial obligations increased as well. In April 1930 the Faulkners bought the old Shegog place, one of the oldest houses in the county, and renamed it Rowan Oak. It was a fine old house, but it was in total disrepair and lacked both electricity and plumbing. The cost of restoring and refurbishing the house was a considerable drain on Faulkner's income, as were the medical bills associated with the premature birth, on 11 January 1931, of Alabama Faulkner, who died several days later. With the birth of Jill Faulkner on 24 June 1933, the Faulkner household now included three children. In addition, after the death of his father in August 1932 and the death of his youngest brother Dean in November 1935, Faulkner contributed to the support of his mother and his brother's wife and child. . . .

Faulkner's Family Problems

Faulkner's fiction of the late 1930s may reflect some of the conflicts he was experiencing in his marriage. In addition to his continuing financial responsibilities, he had found his marriage less satisfying than either he or Estelle Faulkner had expected. At times both Faulkner and his wife drank heavily and argued violently. Living in Hollywood in 1932, Faulkner had become involved with a scriptgirl, Meta Doherty. Faulkner considered divorce, but he was afraid that he would be kept from further contact with his daughter, Jill. Faulkner's preoccupation with the quest for honor in his fiction during these years may well mirror his own search for the honorable choices in his personal life. . . .

Faulkner's Literary Reputation

Now in his mid-forties, Faulkner began spending much time in Hollywood writing screenplays to help alleviate his financial troubles. Although he was doing some fiction writing, six years elapsed between the publication of *Go Down, Moses* and *Intruder in the Dust*. By 1944, his reputation was at a low ebb.

In 1946, however, the publication of *The Portable Faulkner*, edited by Malcolm Cowley, did much to bring Faulkner's work before the public eye once more, and the sale of the film rights to *Intruder in the Dust* for $50,000 in July 1948 helped to alleviate his financial worries. His 1948 election to the American Academy of Arts and Letters was followed by the 1949 Nobel Prize (which was announced in November 1950). Faulkner was now the most respected living American writer. . . .

During the 1950s, Faulkner became increasingly in demand as a lecturer. He made visits for the State Department to such various places as Latin America, Japan, and Greece, and he spoke on college campuses. In 1957, after completing *The Town*, he became writer-in-residence at the University of Virginia and began dividing his time between Charlottesville and Oxford. During these last years of his life he completed *The Mansion* (1959) and *The Reivers* (1962). His interest in flying had faded, but he continued to love riding, especially fox hunting. Beginning in 1959 he suffered a number of serious injuries as a result of falls from horses. A final fall on 17 June 1962 contributed to his already failing health. He entered the hospital on 5 July and died of a heart attack at 1:30 A.M. on 7 July.

Faulkner's Economic Struggles

Joseph Blotner

Joseph Blotner taught at the University of Virginia and other universities. He was the author of an acclaimed biography of William Faulkner and was chiefly responsible for bringing Faulkner to the University of Virginia as writer-in-residence.

The Sound and the Fury *and* As I Lay Dying *brought Faulkner international literary acclaim but did little to put him on a sound financial footing. His time to write to bring in more income was taken up by his need to make livable the old genteel house he purchased in Oxford to provide a place for his wife and in-laws, as well as two servants who had worked for the family for generations.*

But the house had a deteriorated foundation, no electricity, and no plumbing. Faulkner did most of the work himself with the help of family and skilled friends. Records show that in the months of intense renovation, he was not writing or submitting fiction for publication. When he finally had time to write, most of his work was rejected, even as prestigious critics were hailing him as one of the two greatest living American writers, largely based on his earlier works.

In 1844, "Colonel" Robert R. Shegog purchased a tract of land that had been sold eight years earlier by a Chickasaw [Indian] named E-Ah-Nah-Yea, who had received the land as a grant from the U.S. government. Shegog hired William Turner, an English architect, to build a two-story Colonial-style home. They picked an elevated site, the land sloping off around it to bluffs and ravines. The house would face south.

Joseph Blotner, *Faulkner: A Biography*. New York: Random House, 1974. Copyright © 1974, 1984 by Joseph Blotner. Used by permission of Brandt & Hochman Literary Agents, Inc. All rights reserved.

There, seven-tenths of a mile from the courthouse, the land was cleared and the kiln built in which slaves would bake brick for the foundation.

The L-shaped house rose slowly. It was sturdy and roomy, symmetrical in front, with parlors on both sides of the wide entrance hall and a dining room and kitchen extending back from the one on the right. Upstairs were three bedrooms. The Grecian roof of the portico was supported by four tall wooden columns. Above the Georgian front doors was a balcony, and on either side, above the wide, open gallery, were two large shuttered windows upstairs and downstairs. A professional gardener landscaped the grounds, curving a long cedar-lined drive to approach the house.

In 1872, Mrs. Julia Bailey bought the house and much of the land. Over the years, parties of picnickers would follow the paths to the springs in Bailey's Woods. For the boys of Oxford it was a special hunting and swimming preserve, and perfect for games such as hare-and-hounds. When Miss Ellen Bailey died in the house in 1923, Mr. Sally Bailey Bryant inherited it, and rented it to a series of tenants. Gradually it fell into disrepair, and for a time it was vacant. . . .

The Burden of Home Ownership

When Mrs. Bryant learned that William Faulkner was interested in buying and restoring the house, she urged her husband to work something out, even though the Depression made money tight. Will Bryant took to Bill Faulkner, telling him about old times in north Mississippi, about families dead and gone, and about others whose descendants seemed little like their hardy, upright forebears. Finally he told Faulkner he could have the house and four acres of land for $6,000 at six percent interest, with no down payment. He would pay $75 a month. On April 12, 1930, Faulkner signed the papers and the house was his on a deed of trust.

Looking ahead to this new, fixed obligation, Faulkner sent out six stories in the month of April. "Drouth" was one of them, revised now, with the ominous weather symbolic and even contributory to the emotional climate which bred the storm of violence, functioning almost as the weather had in As I Lay Dying....

Pressed for money, he sent out "Selvage" and "Equinox" ("Divorce in Naples" under an earlier title) in May. Both were returned....

Fixing the House

When the Faulkners moved into the old Shegog place in June 1930 ... there was no electricity and no plumbing.... Not far away was the outhouse with its old Sears, Roebuck catalogue [to use as toilet paper]. They would have to use oil lamps and fetch their water from the vine-covered wellhouse.... Faulkner wanted them to have a real home. Years later Faulkner's daughter, Jill, would discern still another motive: it was "the symbol in Pappy's life of being somebody.... Everybody in Oxford had remembered that Pappy's father ran a livery stable, and he had lived in this house up not too far from the livery stable, and this was just a way of thumbing his nose at Oxford.... A nice old house [that] had a certain substance and standing to it." This came through in a letter to Ben Wasson. "I am content and I am happy," he wrote. His new edifice needed a good deal of shoring up, however. There was work for everyone to do, and they plunged into it. The house needed new foundation beams and a new roof, plumbing, wiring, paper, paint, and screens. After a day's work in the July heat, they would go to the wellhouse to take their baths in tandem....

Handy with tools, Faulkner was determined to do as much as he could himself. When he began jacking up the house to replace some of the beams, he got Rusty Patterson to help him. Rusty was a dumpy, good-natured man who came of a good family but chose the life of occasional handyman....

William Faulkner did most of his writing in pen, at a glass-topped table in his home, as shown in this 1955 photograph. © Bettmann/Corbis.

Meanwhile, almost unbidden, the staff was beginning to gather. Uncle Ned Barnett, who claimed he could remember the day the Yankees burned Ripley, took over as general factotum [a servant with various responsibilities]. As butler, he served at the table. As yard man, he milked and also cared for Faulkner's and Malcolm's horses. A man with a feeling for proper dress, he wore a tie when he milked or chopped kindling, and on other occasions he would appear in frock coats inherited from the Young Colonel. Mammy Callie was his opposite number, helping to look after the children and, when she felt like it, creaming butter and sugar for the cakes Estelle would bake in the big wood-burning kitchen range, over which Josie May, the Oldhams' cook, usually presided. Although Estelle often felt that Mammy Callie was more of a nuisance than a help in the kitchen, it was in the natural order of things that she should join the family. She had served Miss Maud and now she was serving her daughter-in-law. As for Uncle Ned, he was simply taking care of another generation of Falkners [as the name was originally spelled]. William Faulkner accepted his role. There was no money for salaries in these early months, but he was responsible for their food, shelter, clothing, health care, and pay when he could afford it. That he should do this was exactly what Mammy Callie and Uncle Ned expected....

If the story-sending schedule is any indication, Faulkner must have spent most of July repairing rather than writing. It was the twenty-fourth of the month before he recorded a submission, when he sent "Red Leaves" to *The Saturday Evening Post*.... the *Post* took this story and paid him $750 for it. Now they could afford to put in electricity, and Estelle ordered an electric stove....

Struggling to Make a Living

Even now his own acceptance rate was not encouraging. Of the thirty-seven submissions he had recorded in the first nine months of 1930, only six had been taken. On the publication day of *As I Lay Dying* he had sent "Never Done No Weeping When You Wanted to Laugh," retitled "That Evening Sun Go Down," to *Scribner's*. They rejected it. Two days earlier he had sent the *Post* "A Mountain Victory." It was straightforward but long: forty-two pages. It was the story of a Confederate officer and his Negro servant, returning home after the war, fatally ambushed by a Tennessee mountaineer. The *Post* accepted the story, but it would be more than two years before it appeared....

When *Scribner's* refused "That Evening Sun Go Down," he sent it to *The American Mercury*. Editor H.L. Mencken liked it, but he was uneasy about Nancy's husband being named Jesus and about her pregnancy being discussed in explicit terms. Faulkner tried to meet Mencken's objections. He did change the man's name. He told Mencken that he kept the dialogue about the pregnancy because "it establishes Judah as a potential factor of the tragedy as soon as possible." Mencken could delete it if he wished. Faulkner did, however, remove the passage about Nancy's swollen belly containing a watermelon that came from somebody else's vine. "I reckon that's what would outrage Boston," he wrote. After further cuts, Mencken printed the story in March 1931....

Little of the Christmas glow persisted into the last days of December. He had not sold a story in over a month, and when he took stock he saw that his total from magazine sales in the last half of the year amounted to only $1,700. One day he went to Mac Reed at the Gathright-Reed drugstore and handed him a small brown velvet bag. "Mac," he said, "can you let me have ten dollars for this?" Mac looked at the $10 gold piece and said, "Surely, Bill." He didn't have that amount himself, so he advanced it from the store cash register. Mac did not ask when the coin would be redeemed, and Faulkner did not know when he could redeem it....

Finally a Little Good News

There were a few encouraging notes. In Sinclair Lewis' Nobel Prize acceptance speech earlier in the month, he had singled out Faulkner for special praise. And a young bookstore owner in Milwaukee named Paul Romaine had written to ask if he could print a collection of some of Faulkner's things from *The Double Dealer*. Faulkner agreed. In the first week of January,

Scribner's returned "The Hound" and "Indians Built a Fence." Associate editor Kyle Crichton wrote that they were "two of the finest stories we have had in months," but that their readers had been complaining about horror stories. But they remembered the story about the spotted horses, and if Faulkner could successfully cut it to 8,000 words, they could take it. They considered him, said Crichton, "one of the greatest writers alive."

Faulkner's Dysfunctional Family

Judith Bryant Wittenberg

Judith Bryant Wittenberg is professor emerita, Simmons College, where she served in teaching and administrative positions. She has published widely on authors such as William Faulkner, Toni Morrison, and Thomas Hardy.

In the following book excerpt, Wittenberg provides insight into Faulkner's dysfunctional family. Faulkner's father, Murry, was dominated by Faulkner's grandfather. Murry failed at the jobs his father found for him, was generally inept and seemed psychologically crippled by the domestic disorder in which he grew up. He had life-long dreams of running a ranch in the West—dreams he was never able to realize. William's parents' marriage began with a romantic elopement, but quickly turned sour. Even on her deathbed, his mother told him that she hoped she would not see her husband in heaven because she never really liked him. William's relationship with his siblings was also acrimonious. He was the eldest, and his father clearly favored his younger brothers, who were bigger, more handsome, and more athletic. The birth of each new brother was traumatic for William because they increased his feelings of abandonment and estrangement.

John Wesley Thompson Falkner [William added the *u* later] (William's grandfather was a less potent figure in the imagination of his fiction-writing grandson than his father, the Old Colonel, and appeared only occasionally in the novels). Nonetheless, he had a strong influence during William's developing

Judith Bryant Wittenberg, "Family Portraits and the Early Years," *Faulkner: The Transfiguration of Biography*. Lincoln: University of Nebraska Press, 1979. Reproduced by permission of the University of Nebraska Press. Copyright © 1979 by the University of Nebraska Press.

years, both directly, as when he taught the boy to drink [liquor], and indirectly, in the recurrence of his difficulties with his son Murry in the struggles between Murry and his own oldest son, William.

Murry's Failure as a Father

Murry, born in 1870, grew to be a tall, strong-jawed, and rather handsome man, but remained very much dominated by his father. Having forced Murry to go to college, for which he had neither desire nor aptitude, the Young Colonel next "allowed" him to take the railroad job which had been his life's ambition, only, in effect, to sell the railroad out from under him. Murry made one inept and futile effort to buy the railroad himself, and then retreated into the role he would play for the rest of his life—that of the ineffectual man whose every move is controlled by his father and who can express his opposition only by failing at most of the jobs his father finds for him. William's rebellion against his father took a similarly passive form for several years, until he discovered his vocation as a writer and until fate, in the form of his father's death, ended his need for denial.

William's Father's Unfulfilled Dreams

Murry's early years were marked by emotional turbulence. His strong-willed and heavy-drinking father was often at odds with his equally strong-willed mother, and the resulting domestic chaos undoubtedly contributed to his volatility and withdrawal. He became taciturn, exhibited a limited capacity to form warm human relationships, and tended to lose himself in hopeless romantic dreams. As one of his sons wrote, in a statement which spoke bitterly, if obliquely, about Murry's failings as a parent as well as about his thwarted hopes, "The only things Dad ever loved were [the] railroad and horses and dogs and the Ole Miss [University of Mississippi] football and baseball teams." Murry was an enthusiastic horseman and an avid reader of pulp Westerns, and long after the responsibility of a wife and rapidly growing family had effectively trapped him in Mississippi, he clung to a desire to go out West, start a ranch, and become a cowboy. It was a project to which his wife, not surprisingly, was fiercely opposed. According to one source, he "never forgave her." . . .

Faulkner's Mother's Unhappiness

One romantically impulsive gesture Murry carried off successfully, his 1896 elopement with Maud Butler. Although the union produced William Faulkner, Murry's personal triumph quickly proved a Pyrrhic [very costly] one, for the marriage was fraught with difficulties. Even on her deathbed long years later, at a time when sentimental reminiscence might have been expected, Maud Butler Falkner looked back upon her marriage with a jaundiced eye, expressing horror at the prospect of being reunited with Murry for eternity and a willingness to do anything in order to attain eternal separation. She and William were talking about "heaven," and she asked, "Will I have to see your father there?" He answered no, and she said, "That's good. I never did like him." Her comment reveals not only her marital disillusion, but also her peppery outspokenness, which was certainly an expression of her independent turn of mind but may also have had a defensive element, first developed by the family upheavals that occurred in her late adolescence. . . .

Strong Grandmother and Mother

Lelia, who came to be known to her grandchildren as "Damuddy" (the name by which the Compson children refer to their grandmother in *The Sound and the Fury*), combined her artistic gifts with imperiousness of manner. Both qualities were passed on to her daughter, in a cycle of repetition like that which marked the Falkner males. Thus Lelia was distraught when she discovered that Maud had married into "that family," because she knew that Murry was a heavy drinker, like his father before him, and for five years she refused to acknowledge the marriage, addressing letters to "Miss Maud Butler, care of Mr. Murry Falkner." ...

Although Maud was a tiny woman who never reached five feet in height, she was sufficiently large in impact, with a vivid and occasionally fierce personality which led one of her grandchildren to describe her as "indomitable." ...

Incompatible Parents

The couple courted for a time and then, during a ride through the countryside one day, impulsively went off and got married, thus starting a pattern of informal quasi elopement that would be repeated by every one of their four sons. They settled in New Albany, a small town not far from Oxford, where Murry was then working as a passenger agent for his father's railroad.

It was a far from ideal combination, and one fraught with the potential for family tensions. Murry was generally withdrawn, but given to outbursts of irrational anger. He was also characterized by a rigidity that demanded, for example, that the noon meal be on the table precisely at twelve o'clock, else he would do an actual about-face and leave the house. Maud was more outgoing, but equally self-contained: a sign in her kitchen, "Don't Complain—Don't Explain," summed up her philosophy. She despised alcohol and criticized those who used it, including her heavy-drinking husband. She had, like her mother, a degree of innate artistic talent and late in life became an earnest painter in the primitive style. She also read a fair amount of serious literature, including the novels of Joseph Conrad, to which she introduced her oldest son, while Murry cared only for westerns, like those by Zane Grey.

The two were thus intellectually as well as temperamentally incompatible and would convey deeply conflicting attitudes to their children. As William published his novels, his mother gradually became a proud champion of her son's talent, while Murry refused to read the work, calling it "trash" and counselling his acquaintances to do likewise. Yet Murry cared deeply for the outdoors, for dogs and horses and riding and hunting, and much of this fervor was communicated to his oldest son. William in turn embodied it in some of his finest writing, from "The Bear" to the horse-race sequences in *A Fable* and *The Reivers*—but not, significantly, until after his father had died. Perhaps because of the sharp division between his artistic mother and his sporting father, William had difficulty in publicly integrating his artist and sportsman "selves," tending to keep the two aspects of his life entirely separate and to play one role or the other at any given moment.

The inauspicious union of Murry Falkner and Maud Butler, likely to provide a troubling environment for any sensitive child, brought forth its first son on September 25, 1897. When it came time to name him, Murry deferred to his father's opinion, as he did in nearly every other area of his life, and allowed the boy to be called after the Old Colonel, changing the middle name from Clark to Cuthbert because the Colonel himself had disliked the former. William, called Billy by intimates throughout his life, was a rather frail baby who suffered from infant colic, which kept him awake during the night for much of his first year, just as insomnia would in his adult years. He early showed physical qualities that identified him closely with his mother and barely at all with his strong-jawed and burly father. From Maud he inherited hooded, brownish black eyes and a small mouth and chin, and like her he would be unusually small as an adult, reaching an eventual height of about five feet, five inches. . . .

The family moved from New Albany to Ripley in 1898, and in 1899, when William was two, his parents' next child, a boy, was born. The second son was always called Jack but was named Murry, after his father. Indeed, he came to look a great deal like his father, tall and heavy-jawed and somewhat saturnine. William became sick after the birth of this baby, and again after the birth of John in 1901, when he was seriously ill with scarlet fever. . . .

Emotionally Threatened

The brothers did prove to be very real emotional threats to the sensitive William. Jack soon received particular attention from his maternal grandmother, who cooked him special foods, and before very long he would surpass his older brother in height; John was a very handsome child, in contrast with the unprepossessing William, and would soon become easygoing and talkative, unlike the silent older child, and a fine athlete whose performances far exceeded William's. These early disparities between Faulkner and his brothers, along with his father's singular hostility toward his oldest son, caused the latter some anxieties, and his fiction strikingly reveals a need to compete with, to assimilate, and, in his fantasy world, to annihilate these troubling competitors. Several of Faulkner's most powerful works contain intense, rivalrous, and destructive sibling relationships, characteristically ending in the death or madness of one of the males. . . .

[In] 1902, at his father's behest and after his futile attempt to buy the railroad, Murry moved his family from Ripley to Oxford into his father's house in order to run the livery stable his father had procured for him. The unwelcome uprooting and the frustration at seeing his dreams of railroading and ranching forever thwarted plunged Murry into bouts of severe drunkenness, storms of rage, and even occasional violence. Not long after he arrived in Oxford, Murry got into a fistfight with a local constable and knocked his opponent through the plate glass window of a grocery store. Maud had by now learned to greet these domestic outbursts with stoic silence and to cultivate a certain detachment. Unfortunately that detachment extended even toward her children, and although

Faulkner ostensibly maintained a good relationship with his mother throughout his life, the portraits of mothers in his fiction reveal his sense that she had failed him in her way almost as badly as had his father....

Personal Losses

For William Faulkner, as he completed his first decade, the losses were multiple, manifested both in actual deaths and in symbolic betrayal.

The deaths were those of both his grandmothers. Near the end of 1906, Granny, his father's mother, became terminally ill with stomach cancer and died just before Christmas....

Another event that year had more serious consequences for the sensitive and introspective child. His mother had been constantly attentive to the dying Lelia during the first half of the year, and her overwhelming grief at her mother's death preoccupied her during the ensuing two months. Then in August she gave birth to her fourth son, Dean Swift, upon whom she bestowed her dead mother's middle names. William had greeted the arrival of the previous two babies by falling ill, and although on this occasion he seems to have avoided sickness, he nonetheless responded to the event as an act of betrayal....

Emotionally Deserted

Though this was a time when William needed maternal attention and reassurance to cope with his grandmothers' deaths, his brother's birth, and the approach of adolescence, he was in effect emotionally deserted by both his mother and his nurse. His yearning for, and sense of betrayal by, these two maternal figures were amplified by this event and emerge in both his later life and his fiction in terms of regressive behavior and problematic attitudes toward women....

The birth of Dean also magnified William's feelings of estrangement from his father, for Murry, who had long been hostile to his oldest son, greeted the baby with joyous acceptance. "He's the best birthday present I ever had," said Murry of the new child, who arrived two days before his own birthday. From the outset he was loving and indulgent toward the boy, readily accepting from Dean the sort of behavior which he would not tolerate from William. This sort of parental favoritism inevitably involves a form of moral injustice which is deeply felt, if not understood, by a child, and there was an especially glaring disparity in Murry Falkner's attitudes toward his oldest and youngest sons. Dean thrived under the indulgent attention of his parents and became a happy and exuberant child who charmed his mother and pleased his father by excelling at sports and the outdoor pastimes that Murry loved. Meanwhile William, though kind and tolerant toward his baby brother, managing to repress his darker responses, became increasingly solitary and withdrawn.

Social Issues in Literature

CHAPTER 2

As I Lay Dying and Family Dysfunction

Faulkner's View of the Bundren Family

William Faulkner

William Faulkner, author of The Sound and the Fury, Go Down, Moses, *and* As I Lay Dying, *spent a year as Distinguished Writer in Residence at the University of Virginia and won the 1949 Nobel Prize for Literature.*

The following excerpt is from a session at the University of Virginia, where Faulkner answered questions about members of the Bundren family. He identifies Jewel as feeling like an alien in the family even though he does not know that he is illegitimate. Darl has always been somewhat insane, Faulkner says, and the funeral journey causes him to fall apart. Whereas Jewel makes it possible for the journey to continue when he sells his beloved horse, Darl tries to bring the journey to a halt by burning down the barn where Addie's decaying body lies. Vardaman is not demented but a thoroughly confused child in a mad world. The story has no villain, Faulkner says, not even Anse, who, like the others, blindly follows meaningless conventions. Darl's insightfulness and poetic nature emerge from his insanity. Addie's unhappiness comes from her unwanted marriage to Anse and her function in his household as a slave.

Mr. Faulkner, in *As I Lay Dying*, did Jewel purchase the horse as a substitute for his mother?

Well, now that's something for the psychologist. He bought that horse because he wanted that horse. Now there was the need to use symbolism which I dug around, scratched around

---

William Faulkner, "Session Fourteen," *Faulkner in the University: Class Conferences at the University of Virginia, 1957–1959*, Gwynn, Frederick L., and Joseph L. Blotner, eds. Charlottesville: University of Virginia Press, 1959, pp. 107–123. Copyright © 1959 by the Rectors and Visitors of the University of Virginia. Reproduced by permission of the University of Virginia Press.

As I Lay Dying and Family Dysfunction

in my lumber room, and dragged out. That was an indication, a simple quick way to show that he did not belong to that family. That he was the alien there. Now just exactly what the connection is between the desire to buy a dangerous untamed horse and to be a country preacher I don't know, but that was the reason for the horse—to show quickly that he did not belong to the rest of the family.

Jewel as the Alien

Can we attach any significance to his letting his father sell the horse later on in the story?

Only that people want to do better than they can do. That this man who loved nothing but that horse would never have believed that he would have sacrificed that horse for anything, yet when the crisis came he did behave better than he thought he would behave. He sacrificed the only thing he loved for someone else's good.

Mr. Faulkner, does Jewel actually know or did he just sense that he is illegitimate?

He don't know and he probably don't care, but his mother knew, and whether she ever—no, she probably never told him. To him it made no difference.

Darl's Insanity

In the same book, was Darl out of his mind all through the book? Or did that come as a result of things happening during the book?

Darl was mad from the first. He got progressively madder because he didn't have the capacity—not so much of sanity but of inertness to resist all the catastrophes that happened to the family. Jewel resisted because he was sane and he was the toughest. The others resisted through probably simple inertia, but Darl couldn't resist it and so he went completely off his rocker. But he was mad all the time.

Is that why he speaks more beautifully than anybody else?

Yes.

Mr. Faulkner, was Darl's motive in burning the barn—is that simply an indication of his madness or was he motivated by his desire to make of no consequence Jewel's sacrifice of his horse in order to get his mother's body to Jefferson?

Probably in Darl's mind that was a violation of some concept, some shape of beauty, to drag that dead putrefying body around any further, and he did the only thing his mad brain could conceive to rid the earth of something which should have been under ground days ago.

Vardaman's State of Mind

Mr. Faulkner, why did Vardaman say "My mother is a fish"?

That was the child, nobody had paid any attention to him. He saw things that baffled and puzzled him, and nobody—none of the adults would stop long enough to show him any tenderness, any affection, and he was groping and that occurred to him that because of the—now, that's another book I should have read, I don't remember exactly what happened, except when he brought the fish home, something that happened from the outside got the fish confused with the fact that he knew his mother's body was in a room and that she was no longer his mother. She couldn't talk or—anyway, suddenly her position in the mosaic of the household was vacant.

Then Vardaman was really—well, he was sane too, it was really just his inability to distinguish illusion and reality that—

That's right. He was a child trying to cope with this adult's world which to him was, and to any sane person, completely mad. That these people would want to drag that body over the country and go to all that trouble, and he was baffled and puzzled. He didn't know what to do about it.

Would you say that Vardaman's love for his mother was the most sincere?

Well, it was because of the child's dependence on his mother, and probably to that child nobody else except the mother paid any attention to him. She was something stable, and his love for her was clinging to something that was stable in his world....

No Real Villain in the Novel

In your novel *As I Lay Dying*, Mr. Faulkner, if there has to be a villain in the story could I be wrong in saying that he was Anse?

I'm not too sure there has to be a villain in the story. If there is a villain in that story it's the convention in which people have to live, in which in that case insisted that because this woman had said, I want to be buried twenty miles away, that people would go to any trouble and anguish to get her there. The simplest thing would have been to bury her where she was in any pleasant place. If they wanted to be sentimental about it they could have buried her in some place that she would like to go and sit by herself for a while. Or if they wanted to be practical they could have taken her out to the back yard and burned her. So if there was a villain it was the convention which gave them no out except to carry her through fire and flood twenty miles in order to follow the dying wish, which by that time to her meant nothing....

Madness, Sensitivity, and Perception

What is the feeling that Dewey Dell in *As I Lay Dying*—what is the feeling that Dewey Dell has towards her brother Darl?

William Faulkner, photographed in 1955, loved horses. During a question and answer session while he was Distinguished Writer in Residence at the University of Virginia, Faulkner discussed the symbolism of Jewel's horse. © Bettmann/Corbis.

She knows without being able to phrase it that he is different somehow from the others through his madness. That maybe he is more perceptive. That he could be more tolerant of her—that is, she knows by instinct that if he found out that she was pregnant it wouldn't make a great deal of difference, but if Jewel found out she was pregnant he would go out and find somebody to kill, and for that reason she knows that Darl is capable of a sympathy, a sensitivity, that won't react in violence to serve an empty and to a woman foolish and silly code, and he is the only one in the family that she could say, I'm pregnant, I'm in trouble, and would get—well, maybe not too much sympathy, but no violent reaction that would merely add more trouble to what she already had.

Mr. Faulkner, as long as we are on Darl, how is it that he could give such detailed description to his mother's death while he is out cutting wood some place else?

Who can say how much of the good poetry in the world has come out of madness, and who can say just how much of super-perceptivity the—a mad person might not have? It may not be so, but it's nice to think that there is some compensation for madness. That maybe the madman does see more than the sane man. That the world is more moving to him. That he is more perceptive. He has something of clairvoyance, maybe, a capacity for telepathy. Anyway, nobody can dispute it and that was a very good way, I thought, a very effective way to tell what was happening back there at home—well, call it a change of pace. A trick, but since the whole book was a *tour de force*, I think that is a permissible trick....

Addie and Maternity

Mr. Faulkner, ... [in] *As I Lay Dying*, Addie says, when she finds she is going to have Cash, "that living was terrible, and that this was the answer to it." Does this mean that this is the confirmation to the fact that living is terrible, or does this mean that she is wrong, that it isn't terrible?

She had probably married Anse because of pressure from her people, but she probably saw through him that he was no good. She was ambitious probably and she married him against her inclination and she saw nothing ahead of her but a dull and dreary life as a slave without—just a slave, no pay, no compensation—then suddenly she found that there was something in motherhood that didn't, maybe didn't compensate for it but alleviated it. That there was some reason for the suffering and the anguish that people, all people, seem to have to go through with. Cash was the first child, and she said to herself, For the sake of this helpless child I can endure. That's what is meant by that, I think.

Faulkner's Characters in an Insane World

William Rossky

William Rossky, who taught for many years at Temple University, was a scholar of diverse interests who published on the English Renaissance as well as on the works of William Faulkner and Mark Twain.

In the following essay Rossky asserts that the continual falling apart of the Bundren family in As I Lay Dying *reveals the meaninglessness and chaos of the world. Darl, who is judged insane, is ironically one of two members of the family who grasps the grim philosophical truth of existence. The other is his mother, Addie. That truth is that we all lie dying even as we walk the earth. Darl and Vardaman long for a home and family and the purpose and connections that are not available to them. Dewey Dell is set adrift by her mother's death. Addie, the iconic center of the family's lives, is a destructive force even in death. She does not consider Anse's children her own and is even hostile toward them. The family is also hurt by the father's egotism, which forces them to desecrate Addie's body by taking her on the long trip to Jefferson. His motive may well be to get a new set of teeth.*

If we look in one direction, toward which William Faulkner himself seems to point, we may see *As I Lay Dying* as a rather simple affair. "I took this family," says the author, "and subjected them to the two greatest catastrophes which man can suffer—flood and fire, that's all." By "subjected them," Faulkner seems here to suggest that the external plot, the

William Rossky, "*As I Lay Dying*: The Insane World," *Texas Studies in Literature and Language*, vol. 4 issue 1, Spring 1962, pp. 87–95. Copyright © 1962 by University of Texas Press. All rights reserved. Reproduced by permission.

Bundrens' meeting and dealing with physical difficulties, is chiefly a testing of human endurance. But the very patterns of reflective internal monologue and of emotional conflict assure us that the story is about more than an encounter with physical hardships. Of what more it consists Faulkner also indicates to us when he tells us that Vardaman is "trying to cope with this adult's world which to him was, and to any sane person, completely mad." *As I Lay Dying* is not only a testing of man but, like the novelist's other most highly regarded works, a testing of the texture of existence. It is a probing which evokes a vision of existence as insane, absurd; of man as little and comic yet capable of a significant, if limited, Quixotic answer to the madness of life. And Darl's terrible laughter ... becomes the keynote of the novel.

The World as Insane

Darl is the seer; his vision is beyond time—the largest in the book. Faulkner himself remarks that Darl, though mad, may "see more than the sane man," and repeatedly the novel confirms this view of Darl.... If he can at times act externally, even conventionally, within the world, he also stands in space where he surveys the whirling globe....

The whole novel conveys the feeling of human motion slowed or stopped; and even the title, perhaps, is meant to convey some sense of this: in life, for all our "terrific" activity, we lie dying.

But if, despite the evidence, which includes Faulkner's statements about Darl, it be objected that we cannot accept a madman's understanding, we have only to turn to the echoes of Darl's vision in other characters to see Faulkner sustaining his refrain. Darl's view of the incongruous world which provides no true "home" for man reverberates sympathetically in Peabody's comment on man's pride as a "furious desire to hide that abject nakedness which we bring here with us," and which we carry with us through life and into the grave. Of course it appears in Addie's belief, even though that belief drives her to wish to live more completely, that "living was terrible," that living is dismally a preparation for dying, and in her perception of the enormous incoherence between "words"—what man in his simple acceptances, slogans, and catchwords believes, or wishes to believe, true—and the complex, often painful reality that "goes along the earth." But it also appears in Vardaman, who, in trying to become a man, attempts pathetically, and for the most part ineffectually, to bring the incongruities of experience together into a meaningful pattern—especially those of life and death—and who dimly sees irrationality in earthly justice: By what justice is he deprived? Because he lives in the country? "I did not said to God to made me in the country. If He can make the train, why can't He make them all in the town because flour and sugar and coffee."

Avoiding Meaninglessness

Most frequently the characters tread cautiously around the edge of Absurdity, sometimes peer over the rim of the canyon, and then withdraw precipitously. In his pity for the child Vardaman, Tull comes close to that edge: "If it's a judgment, it ain't right. Because the Lord's got more to do than that. He's bound to have." "Because He said Suffer little children to come unto Me don't make it right, neither." But Tull sidles only once up to the abyss. He gives it up and echoes Cora's "trust in my God and my reward"; despite his virtues, he generally prefers to remain unconscious, insists that the best thing is not to tax one's brain as Darl does—best to use it "no more than needful." And earthbound as she may be, Dewey Dell knows that woman's "coming unalone is terrible." Even Mosely, the druggist, recognizes sympathetically and ironically that life isn't what it might be, that "life wasn't made to be easy on folks," that, as he suggests, its very difficulty makes people good so that they may die and get out of it. Even Anse sits stunned like a poled steer in dim reaction to the final absurdity, death. But of all those who turn their backs upon the grim reality, Cash, of course, musing profoundly on who in this world are the sane or the insane, comes closest to seeing it clearly—for a moment, indeed, stands with the "fellow in every man that's done a-past the sanity or the insanity, that watches the sane and the insane doings of that man with the same horror and the same astonishment." Cash has here more than a glimmer, but he cannot live long in the consequent "horror and . . . astonishment." Cash, who can put property above morality—"It was either send him to Jackson, or have Gillespie sue us, . . ." and who becomes, as Darl makes clear, a Judas to Darl—"'I thought you would have told me,' he [Darl] said"—is surely not, as some have suggested, the mature point of view of this novel. If at the end, after helping to dispose of Darl, Dewey Dell placidly munches bananas, Cash, though somewhat less callous, also finds a rather easy retreat from complexity in the notion of a gramophone that trickily "shuts up like a hand-grip, with a handle" and somewhat practically contemplates the restful effect of a "little music" after a tiring day's work. As Cash himself says of Darl, "This world is not his world; this life his life." It is the world of Dewey Dell and Cash and Tull who, if they glimpse the abyss, nevertheless veer away lest they see it too clearly.

Mother as Destructive Center

The most prevalent critical view of *As I Lay Dying* is to regard it as a novel of kinship, with Addie acting as psychological center. And whether Addie be considered the center of the novel or not, she is surely a psychological force acting upon the rest of her family. To a degree, at least, the children do react to and complete themselves in terms of Addie's attitudes toward them. Clearly, as Darl indicates, he is motherless and therefore homeless. Through his horse, Jewel acts out not only his intense, near-incestuous love for Addie but also the rage and hostility which the son is apt to feel for the source of his painful conflict. For Jewel the horse is properly a "sweet son of a bitch." If Dewey Dell and Vardaman are incomplete persons, "vegetable" and "idiot," as has often been suggested, perhaps their deficiency may be ascribed to Addie's lack of love for them, although, since Dewey Dell does exhibit feeling, especially in her anguish over the "too soon" on earth which will not even permit her to mourn her mother, and Vardaman is not idiotic but, according to Faulkner, simply a "puzzled" child, how this may be done is perhaps a little obscure....

Cosmic Family Disintegration

The total vision of life, of the universal and terrible incongruities of existence, which is essentially Darl's vision and to a degree Addie's, inspires, then, Darl's sardonic yet poignantly anguished laughter: "'Why do you laugh?' I said. 'Is it because you hate the sound of laughing?'" It is hateful laughter because it rises in a vision of a cosmic absurdity in which the others live almost unaware, the vision of a bitter and painful joke that evokes hysteria. And "Darl. Darl is my brother. Darl. Darl"; and again, "Darl is our brother, our brother Darl." We are all in it—brothers in this sense—yet tragically, bitterly, as the end of the novel makes clear through the treatment of Darl, we are *not* brothers in it. Hysterically, this is what our existence is like. "Yes yes yes yes yes yes yes yes." ...

Anse's Cluelessness as Cosmic

In the light of Darl's understanding, Anse's extremely egocentric interpretation of the universe becomes incongruously funny. Anse sees everything in ludicrously narrow, personal terms. From his toothlessness to the building of the road, all his tribulations are somehow the work of a personally inimical, vengeful something or someone. If it rains, he stands gazing "at the sky with that expression of dumb and brooding outrage and yet of vindication, as though he had expected no less." Or his difficulty is somehow both Addie's fault and due:

"I don't begrudge her the wetting." So comically and limitedly egocentric is Anse's interpretation of the universe that when Cash breaks his leg, Anse says, "But *I* [italics mine] don't begrudge her it." His little obsession in the "original motion," of course, is his new set of false teeth. Even the demonic Jewel, stalking through the novel with his wooden-Indian glare, cracks the seriousness of the novel as, in a ridiculous exaggeration of his code of honor, he helps his horse to preserve its integrity: Says Jewel, rudely refusing a well-meant offer of free feed, "He ain't never been beholden to no man"! And as Darl properly understands, man's psychic thrashings may come ultimately to the comic, as well as serious, fact that Jewel's "mother was a horse." In this framework, Dewey Dell, traipsing up the cotton row and setting an arbitrary magic number of filled sacks to rationalize her venture into the woods with Lafe or trying, so to speak, a hair of the dog that bit her to bring about the abortion, is a highly comic figure—unquestionably here a "mammalian ludicrosity." So too Cash, practical Cash, measures to the half inch everything in the insanely unmeasurable world—he fell, he says, "Twenty-eight foot, four and a half inches, about"—and evades the frightening gambit of thought, which he has himself proposed, by settling for the new gramophone. In the light of the reality of Addie's death, Vardaman's yearning for the red trains on the gleaming track is the comic epitome of all the little desires and postures. They begin early! His somewhat satisfied insistence at the end on the sanity of the family—"Pa and Cash and Jewel and Dewey Dell and me didn't go crazy. We never did go crazy"—is another comic attitude. Vardaman has joined "this world." He will do; dedicated to red trains, he will make out. But the comic stance is perhaps best captured in the tableau at the end of the novel as Bundrens with mouths gaping and half-eaten bananas in their hands are confronted by Anse, his new false teeth, and his new pop-eyed wife. Repeatedly in the Absurdity of the universe, the stasis of little man becomes comic.

Family Conflict and Verbal Fictions in *As I Lay Dying*

John Earl Bassett

John Earl Bassett, president of Heritage University in Washington State, has published books on William Faulkner, Sherwood Anderson, Thomas Wolfe, Mark Twain, and others.

In the following essay, Bassett describes the members of the Bundren family as damaged and in constant conflict. They are both victims and agents of cruelty, beginning with their mother, Addie, who is physically and psychologically abusive, and Anse, a shiftless father and husband, who manipulates Addie and the children, thinking only of his own desires. Dewey Dell, friendless and alone and pregnant with Lafe's child, futilely seeks an abortion. Vardaman wants revenge for his mother's death. Jewel reveals his hatred for his siblings and refuses to be part of the family. Darl, despised by his mother, has no affection for anyone in the family and is betrayed by his father and siblings in the end. And Cash, who struggles all his life for his mother's love, is finally crippled by Darl and Anse who put cement on the bare skin of his broken leg to save themselves time and money.

Addie to many critics is the center of the novel, the most heroic character and the most intelligent. She is also self-centered, cruel, and manipulative. If marriage to Anse is a burden, marriage to Addie is an ordeal. Cora Tull, surprisingly, does reveal Addie's faults. Although pious and self-congratulating, Cora is also a foil to Addie. Another former schoolteacher become housewife, she lacks Addie's intelligence and ability; but her personal fictions provide her a way to live

John Earl Bassett, "*As I Lay Dying*: Family Conflict and Verbal Fictions," *The Journal of Narrative Technique*, Eastern Michigan University Press, vol. 11 no. 2, Spring 1981, pp. 125–134. Copyright © 1981 by Eastern Michigan University Press. All rights reserved. Reproduced by permission.

with her family with affection and care. Vernon Tull, like Armstid and Samson, is a healthy rural husband; and Cora's daughters, if giddy teenagers, are not warped and damaged like the Bundren children. Although she misperceives Jewel's attitude toward Addie, and believes that Jewel is the only child who is "a Bundren through and through," loving nobody and nothing except getting something for the least work, the boy who is Anse's true son, she identifies Addie's flaw—overweening pride. Stripped of its indulgent piety, Cora's analysis of Addie is accurate.

The Cruel Mother

Addie is a lonely woman with too much pride and vanity, so obsessed with violations of herself and her privacy that she is cruel to her family in order to avoid the dangers of affection. She manipulates husband and children as objects to justify her own sanctity, the children to be born in sin mostly out of vengeance or in wedlock as compensation for the sin. She can accept no one as an autonomous identity rather than an object of her needs. She is both the most heroic and the most perverse of all the characters....

Father as Parasite, Not Provider

Every member of the family displays toward Addie a latent hostility that seems caused by a sense of betrayal. As tight with his money as Addie is with her affection, Anse delays calling a doctor, in order to save a few pennies, until it is too late. Though he survives, he is a parasite, not a provider or model for his children. In one way or another he steals from Dewey Dell, Cash, and Jewel. He begrudges the cost of Cash's apprenticeship, even though Cash thereafter brings home income. He self-pityingly complains of Darl being hired out to pay for the road tax, and it is the road—with all it implies about work, change, and motion—that he blames for the disruption of his life. Anse is a creature of words, not action. He can abuse them, to Addie's chagrin. He can fool others into believing he dare not sweat therefore cannot work, and, as Armstid knows, he can "conjure" a man, talk him into almost anything. He can also fool himself with such lines as, "Nowhere in this sinful world can a honest, hardworking man profit". Despite the children he has fathered, however, both his toothless condition and Addie's aggressive denial of their conjugal relationship are signs he is the emasculated as well as the cuckolded husband. Still he fulfills his promise to bury Addie with her father, for the trip offers him a chance to get new teeth and a new Mrs. Bundren.

Dewey Dell

As Anse can restore his manhood, Dewey Dell can destroy her own motherhood. An unwed teenager seeking to abort an unwanted child, she laments her mother's death in a strange way:

> I heard that my mother is dead. I wish I had time to let her die. I wish I had time to wish I had. It is because in the wild and outraged earth too soon too soon too soon. It's not that I wouldn't and will not it's that it is too soon too soon too soon.

Dewey Dell wishes she could wish her mother dead, but her reaction is a function of time. Her nightmare—back "when I used to sleep with Vardaman"—implies she was most unsure about her identity as "a girl" in time. She knew "something was passing" like "wind blowing over me it was like the wind came and blew me back from where it was." The dream of time passing she closely associates with several other images—her first menstruation, Vardaman simultaneously striking the knife into the fish, "the blood gushing," her pregnancy ("the agony and the despair of spreading bones, the hard girdle in which lie the outraged entrails of events"), and the fantasy of striking the same knife into Darl. A dream sequence blurring into fantasy, this passage focuses both her desire for an abortion and her hatred of Darl. Though Vardaman associates his dead mother with a fish, Dewey Dell perceives herself as the mother-fish, whose gush of blood remembered from the onset of menstruation is connected to sexual intercourse and the fetus. In an aggressive reversal she then has the knife to stab her brother Darl, who with his own penetrating eyes has seen into the truth of Lafe's "'picking into your sack.'" . . .

Sister Against Brothers and Father

The sexual significance of her fantasy, however, is not as important as the warped family relations behind it. Darl is in his wordless understanding of her plight as cruel as his own mother. Dewey Dell's revenge on Darl, in fact, seems an outlet for her general hostility toward the family—Mother, Jewel who cares for no one, Anse, and Darl—and toward a male world which has made her an object of contempt. She is the victim of Darl's ridicule, MacGowan's exploitation, Moseley's preaching, Anse's theft, Jewel's anger, and Lafe's lust. If she fulfills the role of woman as betrayer, she does so with as much justification as Faulkner could muster, and thereby as surely as Addie reflects the ambivalence in Faulkner's misogyny.

Vardaman's Revenge

Vardaman is as confused in his hostility as is Dewey Dell. Both also associate Doc Peabody with their dilemma. But whereas Dewey Dell sees him as one who could help her destroy an unwanted child, Vardaman by naive association considers him the villain who has killed his mother. In revenge he releases Peabody's horses, beats them, and sends them galloping out of the neighborhood. Consequently the fish merges in his mind with the horses, or more particularly Jewel's horse, and with his own mother. . . . Vardaman's revenge, like that of the other children, manifests itself in actions which have ambivalent implications.

Jewel's Rebellion

Jewel also recreates his maternal relationship through an animal, one with which he can fight and struggle.... Jewel loves his mother, but he has often showed it by tantrums, sulking spells, and "devilment to devil her." If she loves him it is still Addie-love; if she petted him more, she also whipped him more. She has set brother against brother to her own self-interest. Jewel is the child who is hers alone. As an extension of herself but not Anse, he becomes her weapon. His primary fantasy is not simply of an idyllic love between son and mother on a remote Arcadian hill, but on a hill from which he could be "rolling the rocks down the hill at their faces, picking them up and throwing them down the hill faces and teeth and all by God until she was quiet". It is a destructive love, one in which Jewel has adopted his role as projection of Addie to express her rage against others....

Unloved Darl

Though Jewel may be most often in Addie's mind, Darl is most often in the reader's. Called by some critics an ironic portrait of the artist, Darl is most closely linked to the author by the nature of his substitution for loss of maternal affection....

As the perceiving subject, Darl is drawn towards depersonalization in the act of comprehending and controlling his world. He distances himself from others by vision, but also by almost mathematical conceptions. The very first scene in the book establishes the sibling conflict with the striking image of Darl and Jewel walking single-file toward the cotton house. Darl begins in the lead, but when they emerge from the cotton house Jewel is in front.... Darl like his mother tries to control experience without those words that mislead; and he is also a vain egoist, who dehumanizes the rest of his family, incites shame in Dewey Dell, strips Jewel away from his dying mother so that even if he cannot be there neither can the brother who has Addie's special love.

Fraternal Conflict

Fraternal conflict over the mother in *As I Lay Dying*, however, is not literally between the oldest and a younger brother. Cash is the eldest son, and the only one to resolve satisfactorily the frustration of his love for his mother—through his carpentry work. His ambivalence towards Addie surfaces only twice—first in his obsessively careful work on her coffin and second in his wish to bring back from town a record player, which would bring into the Bundren home an element missing during Addie's life. Jewel recognizes the former when he rages over Cash's noisy licks with the adze. Throughout the early chapters and especially in his single monologue, Jewel frets most not over Darl but over Cash "hammering and sawing on that goddamn box. Where she's got to see him. Where every breath she draws is full of his knocking and sawing where she can see him saying See. See what a good one I am making for you". He also berates Dewey Dell for fanning her, but he doesn't mention Darl, seemingly his true antagonist.

Cash, Jewel says, had as a boy brought Addie dung from the barn as fertilizer for her flowers. He very early worked out a limited non-affectionate relationship with the mother, as Darl did not. Cash and Darl, in fact, seem to be the elder brother doubled in *As I Lay Dying*. Cash is the missing part of Darl's artist-self: the element of craft, organization, common sense that keeps the visionary from self-destructive fragmentation. He is also a more effective replacement for the ineffectual father, since he is the one to direct work around the house and, by hiring himself out as a carpenter, to bring money into the home. Consequently, though lacking the passionate attachment of Jewel to Addie and the strong mental identification of Darl with Addie, he adjusts, albeit as a victim whose twice-broken leg may never fully heal. . . .

As I Lay Dying and Family Dysfunction

Fragmentation of the elder son begins with the implications of the difference between Cash and Darl and culminates in Darl's third-person description of himself en route to Jackson. In fact, it is even Cash, not Dewey Dell or Jewel, whom Darl blames for his betrayal....

The conflict within Darl and the relationship between Darl and Addie dramatize Faulkner's continuing concern with the relationship of son to mother.... Darl complains, "I cannot love my mother because I have no mother."

The Culture of Religious Suppression in *As I Lay Dying*

Nanci Kincaid

Nanci Kincaid is a fiction writer whose works include novels and the short story collection Pretending the Bed Is a Raft.

In the following essay Kincaid says the Bundren family's disintegration comes largely from a culture that teaches a loathing of life and distorts and suppresses human nature. Women especially are taught that the fuller their lives are the more sinful they are and the less likely they are to go to heaven. They are taught to give up life in this world to be happy in the next. So the Bundrens "play dead." Their ordinary lives are full of controls over and suppression of their natures. In this culture even love becomes an empty word, and both mother and daughter are wounded when they give in to love and sex. There is no love in Addie's marriage. Anse has always been emotionally dead and self-absorbed. In the rules they are burdened with, Addie and Dewey Dell become figurative food and shelter for the men in the family.

The South is an exhausted, and exhausting, region—and so it is with our language and symbols. Plumb worn out. But what never seems to wear out is our fascination with our place and our people—and as [critic] Fred Hobson puts it, our consequential "rage to explain."

Notions of Sex and Gender

Faulkner certainly suffers from the rage. His *As I Lay Dying*, written before the depletion of southern symbols and images, doesn't just reinforce the standard—it establishes it. Few white

Nanci Kincaid, "As Me and Addie Lay Dying," *The Southern Review*, vol. 30 no. 3, Summer 1994, pp. 582–590. Copyright © 1994 by Nanci Kincaid. All rights reserved. Reproduced by permission.

southerners can read this work without inwardly shouting, yes, yes, yes, in an orgasmic frenzy—because Faulkner has these people exactly right. We know it. We may hate it, but we know it. We feel it. The Bundrens have been neighbors to us all, if not family. Even now. Because although it's set in the late 1920s, the novel is not about a time.... It is about gender and sexuality and what the South's peculiar brand of Christianity has done to distort our notions of both. Fifty-odd years before Faulkner wrote *As I Lay Dying*, [German philosopher Friedrich] Nietzsche wrote *The Birth of Tragedy*, in which he says:

> From the very first Christianity spelled life loathing itself, and that loathing was simply disguised, tricked out, with notions of an "other" and "better" life. A hatred of the "world," a curse on the affective urges, a fear of beauty and sensuality, a transcendence rigged up to slander mortal existence, a yearning for extinction, cessation of all effort until the great "sabbath of sabbaths"—this whole cluster of distortions, together with the intransigent Christian assertion that nothing counts except moral values, had always struck me as being the most dangerous, most sinister form the will to destruction can take; at all events, as a sign of profound sickness, moroseness, exhaustion, biological etiolation [enfeeblement]. And since according to ethics (specifically Christian, absolute ethics), life will always be in the wrong, it followed quite naturally that one must smother it under a load of contempt and constant negation; must view it as an object not only unworthy of our desire but absolutely worthless in itself.

This is exactly what Faulkner shows us with the Bundren family. We have a region, a culture of people, he says, who have been whipped soundly, nearly beaten to death by the Bible Belt.

Faulkner himself snaps the leather in our ears and lashes out when Addie says, "[M]y father [God] used to say that the reason for living is to get ready to stay dead a long time."

I hear Addie. I know this life on earth is, according to southern myth and Bible-beating, the place where I am supposed to work my way into the next life, the better place, the promised land. And I understand, like most southern women, that the way to live everlastingly in heaven is not to live too happily, or too fully, here on earth. It is not living now that will earn women the right to live later. Addie has gone to her reward. But I'm not that optimistic. It seems like a lot of dead for one spirit to endure, playing dead while on earth, then being dead afterwards. No thanks. I don't want to live getting ready to stay dead. I want to wake up from this sleepy, semiconscious, dreamlike, nightmarelike thing called southern womanhood. When I look out my bedroom window I see Cash, by some other name, hammering away on my casket too. I know he's constructing it with determination. I know he takes pride in his work. I know if I don't wake up and start screaming—soon—I will be laid in that coffin, wearing some party dress I never had occasion to wear here on earth and looking peaceful because the undertaker has sewn my lips into a smile. . . .

The Mississippi terrain in which the Bundrens live is fertile—a lush, green, budding, blooming, rooting, sprouting, swelling, gushing terrain. In fact, it is flooding, an organic overflowing, that keeps Addie Bundren from being promptly buried. The earth seems to yearn, to absorb, constantly soaking up wetness and heat—and from it spring all manner of seeds, pollen, stems, pistils, stamens, blossoms, petals. It is ironic that one of the most fertile regions of the United States would produce a culture of people so tormented by their own fertility—so afraid of it.

Body-loathing is part of self-loathing. Our bodies may be controlled as we control any other animal—Jewel's harnessed horse (although Jewel rides bareback sometimes, he always uses reins); Dewey Dell's milk cow, who moans and begs to be milked, is reluctantly obliged, and afterwards is required to stay behind a locked gate; and even the mules, who are forcibly paired (as in a marriage) and driven into too-deep water pulling a too-heavy load. They drown harnessed together, and after they are dead they float on their backs, legs stiffened and pointing upward like futile phallic symbols drifting downstream.

Love Destroys the Bundren Women

Both Addie Bundren and her daughter Dewey Dell try to acquiesce. They sensibly aspire to be good girl/good woman. It is almost by an accident of nature that they destroy, or at the very least damage, their own lives by becoming sexual—for love.

Addie's sexuality is not a problem within the confines of her marriage, where it is functional, the necessary precursor to childbearing, her duty. Sex without pleasure, without love, is allowed. As long as sex is something Addie does for Anse—and not herself—it is good: "I gave Anse the children. I did not ask for them. I did not even ask him for what he could have given me. That was my duty to him." Addie Bundren, good woman, goes on to say, "I gave Anse Dewey Dell to negative Jewel. Then I gave him Vardaman to replace the child I had robbed him of. And now he has three children that are his and not mine. And then I could get ready to die."

Faulkner understands the capitalistic nature of marital relationships: man as owner/boss, woman as worker/producer, and children as product. As Gayle Rubin says in "The Traffic in Women," "If the total value of the things the worker has made exceeds the value of his or her wage, the aim of capitalism has been achieved. The capitalist gets back the cost of the wage, plus an increment—surplus value." Addie might say, "If the total value of the children a woman bears (and their ability to work) exceeds the value the husband places on his wife in terms of his time, energy, and affection, then he profits nicely." Nobody is ever going to say Addie Bundren cheated her husband out of any property. She steals one child for herself, then pays him three more to make up for it.

Throughout Faulkner's work is the sense that women owe the men in their lives, that men must be compensated for any good thing they do, or even if they never do a good thing. A good woman makes a good man. Her goodness is never a private matter because it determines the goodness of the whole family. The idea is that a region's culture is only as strong as the virtue of its women. Ironically, Anse is always at Addie's mercy, although he never understands that. Anse doesn't seem to understand much of anything: "He did not even know that he was dead," Addie says. But Addie understands. She lives her life getting ready to die, but Anse has always been dead. She says, "[M]y revenge would be that he would never know I was taking revenge."

Addie is never faulted for not loving Anse. But loving a man, clearly not Anse, is the root of Addie's downfall. As with Eve, love is the destructive force in Addie's life, in Dewey Dell's life, in the lives of all women. Love leads women to hell—because love implies sex.

We may assume that when Addie met the preacher in the woods, sex with him was not just a pleasure—to Addie it was a spiritual thing, separated from sin. She says, ". . . waiting for him before he saw me, I would think of him as dressed in sin. I would think of him as thinking of me as dressed also in sin. . . . I would think of sin as garments which we would remove. . . ." As they undressed, they were—momentarily—sinless. Perhaps sex with the preacher only became a sin in Addie's eyes once he deserted her.

The result of this union, the reward and punishment both, was Jewel. He is aptly named. Jewel is the one valuable and beautiful thing in Addie's life. After he is born she spends the rest of her life trying to pay Anse a fair price for Jewel. Addie gets the pick of the litter, but Anse gets four pups to her one.

Dewey Dell, like her mother, will be punished for the sexual expression of her love for Lafe. (We will omit discussion on whether or not Lafe was lovable—an interesting question, as is what Dewey Dell's decision to say yes to Lafe suggests about her. Faulkner, like the region about which he writes, limits women's choices so severely that even to make a wise choice might be impossible.) Whereas Addie's sexuality was suppressed, Dewey Dell's was less suppressed than unestablished. She is the innocent who loses her innocence before she understands what is happening.

Faulkner doesn't present Dewey Dell as sexual, but as childlike. Although she has the responsibilities of an adult, she has none of the small privileges—and none of the small understanding. We understand Dewey Dell's sexuality through Faulkner's erotic language in the scene with the milk cow. It is the Christian idea, and perhaps Faulkner's too, that sex reduces people to the lowest component of their animal natures. Dewey Dell, alone in the barn with the milk cow, says:

> The cow breathes upon my hips and back, her breath warm, sweet, stertorous, moaning. The sky lies flat down the slope, upon the sweet clumps. Beyond the hill sheet—lightning stains upward and fades.... It lies dead and warm upon me, touching me naked through my clothes. I said You dont know what worry is. I dont know what it is. I dont know whether I am worrying or not. Whether I can or not. I dont know whether I can cry or not. I don't know whether I have tried or not. I feel like a wet seed wild in the hot blind earth.

Dewey Dell, a young virgin before Lafe got to her, says she is a "seed." By contrast, Addie says, "I would hate my father for ever having planted me"—suggesting that Addie's seed has taken root, that she is solidly planted in "the hot blind earth."

Women's Names Imply Suppression

The names of the women in *As I Lay Dying* suggest their states of being—their times and places on the road to hell.

Family Dysfunction in William Faulkner's As I Lay Dying

Farmers milk a cow. Faulkner uses cows to symbolize the passivity and usefulness of the female characters in As I Lay Dying, *according to viewpoint author Nanci Kincaid.* © Bettmann/Corbis.

"Addie Bundren" sounds like Added Burden. As if her life is not difficult enough when she is the good woman, the one whose body has been the food and the shelter for all the others, and on whose virtue the reputation of the family depends—even when she is obedient and dutiful and has allowed her aloneness to be thoroughly violated, it is not enough. She must bear the added burden of having loved, been sexual outside her Christian marriage, having borne a son out of her sinful body—which is not hers at all, but theirs, Anse's and her children's. A woman's body does not belong to her, but to her family, her church, her God. Addie exemplifies the Added Burden of a woman who behaves as if her body were her own.

"Dewey Dell," obviously, suggests a fresh morning—and virginal genitalia. Dewey Dell is new to sexuality. Compare the dew of her sexuality with Addie's "water bubbling up and away," "blood strange to . . . other blood," "wild blood boiling," "blood that ran," "cold molasses flowing." Perhaps Dewey Dell's sexuality is innocent only because she does not yet understand blood and violation and a mouth that speaks dead words.

Women Are Shelter and Food

Faulkner's women are not only cowlike in their passivity and usefulness; they are also designed to be inhabited, like houses. Men may enter them anytime they like, and a woman's body houses the man's children as well. Every member of a family has entered and exited the mother's body, though she has entered none of theirs—nor will she ever. This bodily housing of others, whether voluntary or not, sets Addie apart from her family. And when she dies, her only daughter, Dewey Dell, is housing the first member of her own family. The idea of women's bodies as shelters (as well as the relationship between women and houses) is powerful: "A man cannot know anything about cleaning up the house afterward. And so I have cleaned my house," Addie says.

But even more powerful is the idea of women as food. "[T]here was only the milk, warm and calm," Addie says. Breasts offer the first nourishment, the organic link between woman and child that becomes the link between woman and man. Women are the eternal providers of food. Cora Tull bakes cakes. "It is not everybody can eat their mistakes," she says, a line that bears looking into. She goes on to say, "There's not a woman in this section could ever bake with Addie Bundren." Addie has been very good at feeding her family. Upon her death, feeding the family immediately becomes Dewey Dell's job. "I reckon you better get supper on," Anse tells Dewey Dell minutes after Addie dies. "Git up, now, and put supper on.... We got to keep our strength up." Does this mean Dewey Dell is now responsible for Anse's strength "Where's that big fish Bud caught, sister?" Anse asks. "I never had no time to cook it," Dewey Dell says. "You ought to took time," he replies.

In Vardaman's famous chapter where he says, "My mother is a fish," he sets Addie up—even after death—to be eaten by the family. Women readers everywhere are glad Dewey Dell didn't cook the fish. It is significant that Addie becomes a fish: Jesus feeds the masses with multiplying loaves and fishes.

Father and Sons Depend on Mother

I think Faulkner admires women mightily—but his fear of them is equal to if not larger than his admiration. His men may not seem helpless: Cash can build a coffin; Jewel can break a horse; Vardaman can catch a fish—but none of them can eat regularly—without a woman. They can't provide their own nourishment. Anse might have dropped the seed in the field, but a mule plowed the row, and Addie and Dewey Dell took the crop and shucked it, peeled it, snapped it, washed it, canned it, and cooked it. It was the women who turned the crop into food. Who will feed Anse and his boys now?

Worse luck, Anse has lost his teeth. It's an abhorrent physical image: Anse is a toothless old man with a name that sounds like ass or anus and a mouth that—toothless—now looks like an ass or anus. Does Faulkner mean everything that comes out of Anse's mouth is waste—all his Christian platitudes?

Toothlessness is an infantile quality. It suggests helplessness. Mothers nurse babies until the babies get teeth—and are able to bite. Anse has no bite left. His mouth cannot rip or tear or shred. It cannot grip. Toothlessness is a radical impotence. Anse can only ingest soft things, and who will make things soft for him once Addie is dead? Isn't it the job of women, with their pillowlike bodies, to soften the world for men?

Maternal Influence in *As I Lay Dying*

Marc Hewson

Marc Hewson, professor of English at the University of Ottawa, has written on William Faulkner and Ernest Hemingway.

Addie is the central figure in the novel though she dies early in the story. She is the "I" of the title, the reason for the journey in the book, and the central figure in the lives of her husband and children. Hewson sees her major impact in leading her sons to reject their father's paternal values which deny females' life, action, and motion. The male view also negates human relationships. Anse, Addie says, is always dead, emotionless, and without meaningful connections to others. In motherhood, Addie finds life, a purpose in this otherwise meaningless existence. Each child adds to her life. Vardaman, the youngest, is the only one who is unable to accept her death. He inherits her belief in action as he drills holes in her coffin to give her air. Jewel and Cash also show their feelings for her in actions, rather than words.

Addie functions as the almost absent center of [*As I Lay Dying*]. Figuratively, she is the impetus behind the trip to Jefferson since it is her dying wish to be returned to her people and buried alongside them that forces the venture. Literally, she is centered by reason of her single monologue and its placement, though admittedly her chapter falls somewhat after the true midpoint and so does not neatly divide the book in

---

Marc Hewson, "My Children Are of Me Alone: Maternal Influence in Faulkner's *As I Lay Dying*," *The Mississippi Quarterly*, vol. 53 no. 4, Fall 2000, pp. 551–658. Copyright © 2000 by The Mississippi Quarterly. All rights reserved. Reproduced by permission.

two. . . . At least part of that story is the demonstration of Addie's influence on her sons, her training of them to fight the patriarchal world view embraced and exemplified by their father, Anse.

The Feminine and Maternal Principle

Through the process of Addie's monologue and the combined actions and thoughts of her children, the dynamic feminine and maternal principle which she maintains negates the stolid and unmoving male principle, and Addie herself becomes a possible source of female power in the book. . . . By making her children extensions of herself, she refuses to validate the masculine dominance which attempts to silence her. The trip to Jefferson thus becomes for her boys a form of education in her ways. By mourning her and contemplating their relationships with her, Cash, Darl, Jewel, and Vardaman learn to emulate her and adopt her suspicion of patriarchal constructs. . . . In other words, a new order is being established by the taking of Addie's body to be interred, one based on her teaching rather than Anse's.

Actually, Faulkner sets up the dichotomy between masculine and feminine world views early on through Addie's relationship with Anse. When we first see him, Anse is sitting almost motionless, rubbing his hands together and wondering whether the middle two boys can make a wood-loading trip before Addie dies. He is worried that if they do not come back with the wagon quickly it will spoil Addie's plans to start the trip to Jefferson as soon as she dies. Anse knows that "she'll want to start right away," that "she'll be impatient" to begin. Part of the worry, though, is based on Anse's natural dislike and suspicion of the dynamism which he credits to his wife, and which is juxtaposed to his own tendency towards entropy [degeneration]. Although he warns the boys to be swift because he "would not keep her waiting," most of his married life, as we later learn, has been spent doing just that, stymieing Addie's growth and keeping her still.

Female Action and Male Inaction

With this example of ill-matched partners in place, Faulkner goes on to broaden the categories beyond the personal. In Anse's first monologue the difference between masculine stasis and feminine process is being defined. The always shiftless Anse curses the road which comes "right up to [their] door, where every bad luck that comes and goes is bound to find it." In Anse's speech, roads, horses, and wagons are always symbols of feminine motion which challenge masculine authority. He believes that man was meant to stay put, not roam the earth, that God never "aimed for man to be always a-moving and going somewheres else." If He had, Anse asks, "wouldn't He a put him longways on his belly, like a snake?". As far as Anse is concerned, since man was made on the vertical axis like trees and houses, God must have meant him to remain stationary. Thus when he "told Addie it want any luck living on a road when it come by here.... she said, for the world like a woman, 'Get up and move, then'". The confluence of divinity, serpents, and the evils of motion begins to make clear the vehemence of his hatred of the feminine principle which he attributes to Addie. To his mind, the argument between moving or acting and staying still is one which the male side should always win.

However, Anse fails to realize that his symbology is based on the primacy of the female image, that, without the feminine body (land or woman) out of which they rise, men and trees could not exist. What this means is that Anse inadvertently privileges Addie's position.... And surely, this is a novel characterized less by trees and houses (or perhaps by men, for that matter) than it is by roads, wagons, and horses. It is important to note, for example, that even after her death Addie continues her activity by forcing the trip. More to the point, though, her activity will continue through the example she has set for her children and which they emulate throughout the journey.

The dichotomy between female activity and male inaction that is sketched out at the book's beginning is more fully fleshed out and reaches even higher stakes by the time Addie's monologue arrives. No longer merely a dispute between action and passivity, between uprooting lives and putting down roots, it is now a battle between life and death. For the most part, Western society envisions life as a movement from womb to grave, an active development which devolves into stasis only at death. However, the masculine ideal in *As I Lay Dying* inverts this generally accepted wisdom by linking inertia not only with death but also with life. More than just being a refutation of activity and living, the patriarchal philosophy questions even the possibility of meaningful existence, claiming, in the words of Addie's father, "that the reason for living was to get ready to stay dead a long time". It is of course Anse who is the most obvious example of this theory in practice. As an emulation of or training for death, life is static for Anse. Thus it is only a dogged adherence to duty (not least because it offers him living martyrdom) and not love or marital honour which makes Anse so quick to comply with Addie's final wishes. Essentially, by accepting Addie's ultimatum, he is rehearsing the male idea that life is deathly.

Patriarchal Negation

Needless to say, Addie's fidelity to an active understanding of existence causes her to resent and defy such a philosophy. This is due to her intuitive knowledge of the real dangers of such an outlook. To be sure, the patriarchal life view negates female power out of hand. More importantly, though, it negates the importance of human relationships. As Anse's example suggests, the life-as-death-model denies the need for interaction. This is the reason Addie claims that Anse is already dead, even if he is not aware of it—for her death means the absence of heartfelt communication and relation to other people. That Anse trades her corpse for a new wife and new teeth in Jefferson reflects the paucity of emotion in the male system and the effective emptiness of the relationships developed under it. As a possible escape from this static living death, as a way of finding meaning in life, Addie tries various methods of relating to others, first through her career as a teacher, then through her marriage to Anse.

Motherhood Teaches Addie About Life

It is only with motherhood, though, that Addie discovers the lie which, both her father and Anse tell her. While her other attempts fail, she is able to find life and union through her children. Perhaps retaining certain of her father's notions, she still believes "that living was terrible." However, she realizes that motherhood "was the answer to it," a palliative for existence, or at least for the male view of existence, and it provides Addie with knowledge she did not have before about life....

Addie's understanding of motherhood's power and blessing is furthered by her realization that multiple children do not divide a mother's love but that each successive child is subsumed into the loving union. As Addie soon perceives, despite her initial anger at Anse for impregnating her again, the bond between her and Cash is not weakened by Darl's birth: "I was three now". Far from breaking the ... bond between Addie and Cash, then, Darl's birth reconfigures the relationship to create a triad. This idea of proliferation without division is an important element in Addie's construction of identity.... In a sense, each child becomes Addie writ small, and it is through each that she is reincarnated in the novel, so to speak. As her name implies, Addie is redoubled by each new child, to the extent, even, that the three children whom she claims belong solely to Anse (Darl, Dewey Dell, and Vardaman) remain hers and emulate her views. Through their individual characterization, as well as through their interaction, Faulkner provides a composite Addie, a set of maternal ideas and ideals to counter and perhaps overcome the negative patriarchal view that Anse and Addie's father embody. . . .

Vardaman's Grief

It is arguable that Vardaman, the youngest child by some years, learns least from the trip, given that he is the least able to accept his mother's death. The only son present in her final minutes, he is also the only one who cannot believe it. Indeed, Vardaman is unable to express the loss of his mother in words at all. After her final breath, he peeks around Anse's leg, "his mouth full open and all color draining from his face into his mouth, as though he has by some means fleshed his own teeth in himself, sucking". Though it is the focal point, his mouth remains unable to articulate his emotions, and he backs out of the room quickly and silently, the horror of his loss more poignant perhaps for its inarticulability. Yet while the funeral procession itself teaches him less about Addie than it does the others, Vardaman may be said to learn most from Addie's death. . . .

The reason Vardaman is a failed speaker lies in the fact that words are powerless for him because they are arbitrary. Faulkner underscores this arbitrariness for us through Darl's repeated taunt later in the novel that "Jewel's mother is a horse" and Vardaman's inability to understand how brothers can have different mothers. If Jewel's mother is a horse, Vardaman begins to quiz his brother, "then mine can be a fish, cant it, Darl?" However, the capriciousness of symbols starts to worry the boy. He knows that Jewel is his brother, and therefore assumes his own mother "will have to be a horse, too". . . .

Ultimately, though, Vardaman's puzzlement over language, his birthright from Addie, is perhaps less important than his propensity for action, something he holds in common with his brothers. His attempts to save Addie by catching the fish

As I Lay Dying and Family Dysfunction

Mules pulling a wagon in 1942. Viewpoint author Marc Hewson explores the symbolism and significance of the mule-drawn wagon used to carry Addie's body to burial in As I Lay Dying. © Wallace Kirkland/Time Life Pictures/Getty Images.

and, more tragically, by taking Cash's augur to her coffin lid are similarly based on his love for her. Just as Darl tries to burn down Gillespie's barn to prevent any further humiliation of Addie's corpse and Cash carefully constructs the coffin out of concern for her comfort, Vardaman tries to express his emotions through actions rather than words. Addie's example of non-linguistic love becomes the basis of Vardaman's actions, and the confusion expressed by his words and thoughts lends credence to the conclusion that, in this novel at least, actions speak clearer if not louder than words.

Love Shown by Works, Not Words

Jewel's love for Addie may also be said to be based more on doing than on saying. Certainly his feelings are more complicated than Vardaman's, not merely because of his age but also because of the barely submerged knowledge of his paternity. Of course, the dynamic feminine principle which Addie espouses is as much his inheritance as it is Vardaman's. Like her, Jewel dislikes inaction; just as her mind is set on beginning the journey immediately after her death, so is her son's. That eagerness, as well as his own inarticulable grief, emerge in Jewel's impatience with Darl and with Cash's slowness in carrying the coffin to the wagon, which prompts him to attempt to maneuver it singlehandedly. As Darl describes it,

> Jewel will not wait. He is almost running now and Cash is left behind.... I am not even touching [the coffin] when, turning, he lets it overshoot him, swinging, and stops it and sloughs it into the wagon bed in the same motion and looks back at me, his face suffused with fury and despair....

It comes as little surprise, then, that Jewel has such a fierce attachment to his horse (another of Anse's symbols of female movement). Indeed, there is a similarity between Jewel's treatment of the horse and his treatment of Addie. Towards both he exhibits a gruff, almost abusive, love. Early on he calls the animal a "sweet son of a bitch," and, while trying to calm it before feeding it, he stands "with dug heels, shutting off the horse's wind with one hand, with the other patting the horse's neck in short strokes myriad and caressing, cursing the horse with obscene ferocity". There is a similar coarseness in his calling Addie's grave "a damn hole in the ground", but one which stems more from despair at her death and the ensuing indignity of the trip than from a true animosity toward her. The fact that Jewel refuses Anse's order to leave his horse behind becomes a powerful reminder of the complex relationship that he and Addie shared and of his denial of his father's views. Certainly not "a deliberate flouting of her", as Anse calls it, Jewel's decision to ride his horse seems appropriate to the sort of relationship the mother and son shared.

Darl Is Most Like Addie

Insight into his siblings does not lead Darl to a sensitivity toward them. Indeed, his knowledge of Dewey Dell and Jewel is openly hostile. However, his maliciousness almost matches Addie's in her 'desire to revenge herself against Anse for making her pregnant with Darl. The initial betrayal she feels at Anse's destroying the dyad of mother and only child is mirrored in Darl's feeling of betrayal by a mother who seemingly refuses him love. This similarity of temperament is underscored by Cora Tull's belief that Darl is "the only one of them that had his mother's nature, had any natural affection". Cora's statement is not wholly accurate, of course. Darl is often less than affectionate to his family, and, as we have seen, the other children also retain much of Addie's nature. What is more, his own statement that "it takes two people to make you" denies Addie's claim that "[m]y children were of me alone". Darl's obsession with paternity stems from his bitterness that even an illegitimate child like Jewel seems more loved by Addie than he is. Yet in truth he might be the child who gains most from being Addie's son and suffers least from being Anse's, his eventual incarceration in the Jackson asylum notwithstanding (though even this might be considered a sort of blessing in disguise). In many ways, then, he is the child most like Addie, as Cora imagines. Certainly Faulkner takes pains to confirm some bond between them in the form of their shared attachment to the earth.

Addie's earthiness is echoed most obviously in her alignment with the horizontal principle of movement and its corollaries, like the road which lies "flat on the earth" before the Bundren home. The kinship goes deeper than a mere propensity toward activity, however. As she points out in her monologue, Addie considers herself to be a part of the land; not only does she cling to it by doing but she also becomes it, or rather it becomes her after she gives birth. She lies beside Anse in bed, "hearing the land that was now of [her] blood and flesh". In a way, then, Addie indeed is the earth-mother that some critics have dubbed her. At least part of the reason for living as far as she is concerned is "the duty to the alive, to the terrible blood, the bitter red flood boiling through the land," and she begins to view her children as also being products of this junction of earth and woman: "My children were of me alone, of the wild blood boiling along the earth".

Darl is the child who most manifests this connection, as even the other Bundrens make plain. Early on in the novel, he is twice characterized in terms of the landscape surrounding him. Dewey Dell describes him sitting "at the supper table with his eyes gone further than the food and the lamp, full of the land dug out of his skull and the holes filled with distance beyond the land", almost as if he is himself made of the earth around him and somehow projects out of it. Anse, too, in a rare moment of insight, figures Darl as linked to the earth, "his eyes full of the land". Like Addie, Darl is both encompassing the land and enthralled by it (or in thrall to it, Anse fears), and it is just this connection which begins to steer him away from his father's teaching: ". . . he was alright at first, with his eyes full of the land, because the land laid up-and-down ways then; it wasn't till that ere road come and switched the land around longways and his eyes still full of the land, that they begun to threaten me out of him".

Feminine and Maternal Rebellion in *As I Lay Dying*

Amy Louise Wood

Amy Louise Wood, professor of history at Illinois State University, is the author of Lynching and Spectacle.

In the following selection, Wood asserts that the character Addie is a powerful person, a rebel, an enigma, and the center of the novel As I Lay Dying. *Through her roles as mother and adulteress, she rejects society's oppressive views of woman's subservience. Her rebellion is scarcely visible, however real it is internally. Her physical side confirms her reality at the same time that she rejects her father's religious views of an afterlife. Her world is the here and now, and she craves both pleasant and painful human connections to make her feel alive. Her marriage to Anse fails to bring her that relationship. Though having a child brings her a true relationship with another human being, she refuses to be a dutiful, selfless mother and follows her own whims in favoring one child over another. The idea of maternity is repeated in the pregnant Dewey Dell, but it has the opposite effect on Addie's daughter, making Dewey Dell feel more alone.*

Addie Bundren uses her body to rebel against her society, establishing meaning through the physical pains and pleasures of her nurturing motherhood and selfish sexuality. Yet, she does so neither by removing herself from her society nor by deconstructing it. Rather, she embraces her roles as mother and as sinning adulteress, and ... she manipulates and distorts those roles and their meanings to expose her society's empty constructions of motherhood, love, religion, and lan-

Amy Louise Wood, "Feminine Rebellion and Mimicry in Faulkner's *As I Lay Dying*," *The Faulkner Journal*, vol. IX no. 1, 2, Fall 1993, pp. 99–112. Copyright © 1993 by The Faulkner Journal. All rights reserved. Reproduced by permission.

guage, creating a sense of self and negotiating power for herself separate from them. It is through this process that she is able to lay down her life and tell her story.

Transcending Yet Affirming Femininity

By merging her motherhood and sexuality together as a mode of self-expression, Addie transcends societal expectations of femininity. Yet by having her find meaning in her life through her body, Faulkner is reaffirming cultural notions of femininity....

In this context, Addie Bundren engages in a powerful form of mimicry. By forming her identity through her body, both as mother and as adulteress (whore), she conforms to cultural gender constructions, without allowing her rebellion to be visible. Yet she manipulates the roles of mother and whore, affirming the pleasure and power they bring her....

Addie Bundren ... reclaims and affirms her own body, for only through passionate physical connections to other people does Addie feel alive and connected to her body. Through these connections, Addie constructs a feminine notion of being that counters the masculine reason for being posited by her father, who said, "The reason for living is to stay dead a long time". In rejecting her father's credo, she is, likewise, rejecting the Christian notion that one suffers during one's secular life for the promise of a better life in the afterworld; instead, Addie searches for passion and feeling in this world. The reason for living is then grounded in living itself, in feeling and doing, which Addie calls "the duty to the alive". For Addie, existence is only meaningful if it is experienced physically, not only in pleasure but also in pain.

In the beginning of her monologue, Addie speaks of her hatred and bitterness because she feels disconnected and so insignificant to those around her. As a schoolteacher, she beats the children to feel and see their blood, so that by physically feeling her, they will know her. She thus violently forces a merging of self and other, thinking, "Now you are aware of me! Now I am something in your secret and selfish life, who have marked your blood with my own for ever and ever".

Addie also feels alienated from her own primal, natural self, hating her father for "having ever planted" her. Beating the children, then, also allows her to sense her own blood and body, thus validating her own existence: "When the switch fell I could feel it on my own flesh; when it welted and ridged it was my blood that ran . . .".

Alone but Connected

Her marriage is another violent and aggressive attempt at connection. Articulating her decision to marry—"and so I took Anse"—Addie conceptualizes her marriage as a primarily physical experience, while appropriating masculine language of sexual possession. Yet when she marries, she feels further disconnected from herself and the feeling of being alive. Even sex in marriage never made her feel her "aloneness violated," the feeling of primal connections, "not even by Anse in the nights".

Her aloneness does become violated, however, when she has her first child, when motherhood and nursing make her feel connected to another being and her own body. . . . It is as if her sense of personal wholeness is disrupted by the primal connection of nursing, but at the same time that physical intrusion by another is what enables her to experience an integrated sense of self. In this way, she nurtures her motherhood, using it to fulfill her own need for wholeness within the construction of nurturing and selfless maternity.

Addie is thus selfish in her motherhood, as she rejects the notion of maternal self-sacrifice and duty. While her neighbor Cora, often the voice of community and Christian standards, envisions a mother as a silently suffering and selfless receptacle of her husband's children, claiming, "I have bore what the Lord God sent me", Addie says "My children were of me alone". Motherhood is not a "duty" for Addie, but an experience for her pleasure and feeling, as she favors some children and rejects others....

Addie not only suckles Jewel but mourns and weeps for him as well, for when Addie realizes that by purchasing a horse, Jewel has deceived her, Darl says that he finds her "sitting beside the bed where he was sleeping in the dark. She cried hard".... Yet Addie is not crying over her son's corpse but over his replacement of her with a horse—a selfish mourning. Again, Addie embraces a social conception of femininity and distorts it to suit her own purposes....

Hating Deception and Convention

Addie inverts the word "sin" so that it takes on a positive and creative meaning for her. Words such as "terrible" and "violation" also becomes positive in Addie's consciousness, as they signify passion, power, and feeling. Likewise, although Addie says that names do not "matter," she loads Jewel's name with meaning. Reappropriating and manipulating language becomes a means for Addie to negotiate power for herself within a culture she finds stifling and "dead."...

Addie hates deception above all else, and, as Darl says, "tried to teach us that deceit was such that, in a world where it was, nothing could be very bad or very important...". As Paul Nielson argues, Addie feels that when words are devoid of doing or feeling, they deceive and so are meaningless. Thus she breaks down and cries, not only when she realizes that Jewel, by running off nights to buy the horse that displaces her, was deceiving her, but when she realizes as well that, by keeping his paternity secret and by manipulating and inverting language, she has been deceiving him....

Likewise, in wanting to be buried with her father in town, Addie resolves her hatred and reconnects with the paternal body that "planted" her. At the same time, her desire to be

As I Lay Dying and Family Dysfunction

William Faulkner and his wife, Estelle, at their home near Oxford, Mississippi, in 1955. In As I Lay Dying, Faulkner explores women's conventional roles as wives and mothers. © Bettmann/Corbis.

buried in town, away from her husband, is her most visible and outrageous rebellion, for, as Cora exclaims, "a woman's place is with her husband and children alive or dead". And by forcing her family on a journey in which, faced with her rotting, smelling body for days, each member must take account of her body and their relationship to it, Addie makes her final mark and most significant difference in life.

Dewey Dell and Addie

Her death requires each of her children to enter into and find a place for himself or herself in culture. Yet while each of Addie's sons must find a masculine identity for himself, her only daughter, Dewey Dell, repeats Addie's struggle into womanhood. Through her pregnancy, Dewey Dell is thrown back into the semiotic bond, the instinctual drive that reconnects her to her mother upon her mother's death....

Like Addie ... she relates to the world physically, through touch rather than words. Dewey Dell retains a physical connection to her mother that in her brothers is denied or displaced, wiping Addie's brow and fixing her covers on her deathbed. She grieves for Addie by throwing herself on top of her, "clutching her, shaking her with the furious strength of the young"—her grief made more potent by the fact that her mother dies as Dewey Dell's own body is changing with the onset of motherhood, which, since she is not prepared for it, becomes *"the agony and the despair of spreading bones"*. She is also uncomfortable and self-conscious about her soon-to-be obvious sexuality, as she imagines Darl undressing her with his eyes, noticing her unvirgin state.

Although, unlike Addie, her sexuality and motherhood make her feel disconnected and outside of herself, she, like Addie, struggles to find a sense of herself through bodily connections with others. She conceives her maternity and her "unvirginness" in purely physical terms....

Just as she uses her mother's word, "dead," to describe the world, she also appropriates her mother's words, "terrible" and "unalone" to describe primal connection....

In the same way, while Addie finds power in motherhood and sexuality, Dewey Dell feels isolated and disconnected. She, unlike Addie, is not able to meld her sexuality and her motherhood together, for she cannot resolve the notion that she is pregnant by the man she desires. Indeed, while Addie nurtures her illicit motherhood, Dewey Dell wants to abort her pregnancy, so that she would "be all right alone". While Addie is aggressive in her sexuality, Dewey Dell passively submits. She feels the power coming from her passions and her body, yet feels trapped within her femininity, lost like "a wet seed wild in the hot blind earth".

Dewey Dell does, however, as Doreen Fowler has argued, complete Addie's revenge against patriarchal culture, becoming, along with Jewel, "the chosen avatars of maternal fury". According to Fowler, Darl seeks to enact the ritual murder of his mother, by drowning and then burning her body, in order to separate himself from her and enter into patriarchal culture. Dewey Dell's attack on Darl at the end of the journey avenges not only the desecration of Addie's body but the silent torments and taunts he has inflicted on Dewey Dell. The novel ends with Dewey Dell, her abortion denied, sitting atop the family's wagon, eating bananas, emerging as the representation of maternal culture. Thus, as Deborah Clarke has pointed out, despite Addie's death and burial, "the mother's body ultimately cannot be vanquished". Indeed, Addie's body persists as the most vivid and powerful presence in the novel.

Father as Victim as Well as Villain

Rita Rippetoe

Rita Rippetoe is an independent scholar and author of Booze and the Private Eye: Alcohol in the Hard-Boiled Novel.

Most scholars, with little qualification, have been critical of the patriarch in As I Lay Dying *as lazy, parasitical, unimaginative, and self-absorbed. Rippetoe acknowledges this in the following selection and then places Anse in a slightly different light, as a victim of poverty and physical afflictions. Reference is made in the novel to Anse's earlier sunstroke which, Rippetoe finds, can result in an ailment called anhidrosis. Victims of this disorder are afflicted with both physical and mental problems, including dementia and changes in personality. In addition, Anse's lack of teeth and foot deformities (resulting from an accident when a load of wood fell on him) are meant to form a picture of an old man's losing battle with poverty in the Mississippi countryside where the only available doctor probably had no medical degree. Thus Anse's faults—his insensitivity, greed, and manipulation of his children—have to be regarded in light of his poverty.*

Anse Bundren of *As I Lay Dying* has been described by critics in largely negative terms.

Irving Howe is perhaps easiest on Anse in terming him an example of the "universal comic type, the tyrannically inept schlemiel whose bumbling is so unrelieved and sloth so unalloyed that he ends by evoking an impatient and irritated sympathy." Cleanth Brooks, in contrast, calls him "one of Faulkner's most accomplished villains" and rails against his

---

Rita Rippetoe, "Unstained Shirt, Stained Character: Anse Bundren Reread," *The Mississippi Quarterly*, vol. 54 no. 3, Summer 2001, pp. 313–326. Copyright © 2001 by The Mississippi Quarterly. All rights reserved. Reproduced by permission.

As I Lay Dying and Family Dysfunction

ability to "survive blasts that would kill more sensitive organisms . . .". Robert Kirk claims that Anse "lacks even the elemental type of imagination that would make such trickery possible: indeed his indolence stems chiefly from this lack of imagination. He would occasionally do something helpful if he knew what to do and how to do it, for the strongest force in Anse's character is a misty, half-formed desire to function in some way." Andre Bleikasten, in his comprehensive study of Faulkner's *As I Lay Dying*, presents a number of opinions on Anse. On one hand he sees Anse as "the great comic creation of the novel." He then grants that Anse occasionally achieves tragic stature, but immediately undermines this admission by referring to Anse as "a farcical latter-day Job." Bleikasten takes Anse's laziness as a given and adds to it the sins of hypocrisy, egotism, avarice and callousness, while cautioning the reader that the comic touches which Faulkner gives his portrayal almost allow the reader to forget how despicable the character is. Yet, in a footnote to the accusation that Anse is a weak husband, Bleikasten comments on Anse's lack of teeth as symbolic castration, and admits that the trip to Jefferson may be a "parodical reconquest of manhood, following the matriarchal reign of Addie, the 'castrating' wife and mother". . . .

Anse's Physical Ailments

Each of these critics has made an able case for his or her interpretation of Anse's actions and words. Yet it seems that something is missing from the critical picture, that some vital clue, lying neglected or barely noticed, would convert Anse from Brooks's human buzzard to a fully realized human being. Within the text of the novel stands the symbolic text of Anse's body: deformed, deprived and physiologically afflicted by disease and accident, this body/text is inscribed by poverty. Following the clues provided by Faulkner's physical description will lead to a consistent and believable Anse whose actions, though still incompatible with his proclaimed motives and still less than admirable, are comprehensible to the reader. This Anse is not a generalized stereotype of a poor Southern white male, a shiftless hillbilly, but rather a man whose character, as well as his body, has been distorted by the effects of specific afflictions....

Anse's Physical Ailment

Most critics see Anse's lack of sweat as a symptom or a symbol of ingrained laziness....

Faulkner seems set on convincing the reader that Anse does not sweat. Darl tells us: "There is no sweat stain on his shirt. I have never seen a sweat stain on his shirt". Vernon Tull confirms this observation: "Except for the lack of sweat. You could tell they [Anse's shirts] aint been nobody else's but Anse's that way without no mistake". Since neither Darl nor Vernon seems inclined to make excuses for Anse, we may regard their joint testimony as proof that Anse does not sweat in a normal fashion for the climate in which he lives. The usual reading of Anse's lack of sweat as the result of his indolence defies logic.... Based on this climatological data, one can conclude that, without air conditioning, any normally constituted person, no matter how inactive, will sweat frequently in the course of a lifetime near Oxford, Mississippi. Yet two separate and unrelated witnesses assert that Anse does not sweat enough to stain the material of his shirts.

Suppose we reverse the reasoning that Anse does not sweat because he does not work, and that he does not work because he is lazy. What if the opposite is the case: Anse cannot work because he cannot sweat. Inability to sweat is a medical condition known as anhidrosis. Sweat is necessary to help cool the body and its absence is a symptom worth noting....

In lay terms, a person who cannot sweat will suffer from frightening, uncomfortable and dangerous symptoms when exposed to heat, symptoms which will be increased by exertion and which can lead to death.

If Anse had been a lifelong sufferer from anhidrosis, it is unlikely that he would have been able to prepare to court Addie by building a new house. But we have already been informed that Anse's problem dates from the age of twenty-two, when he took sick, i.e. suffered heat stroke. The average person may think of an attack of heat stroke as a temporary inconvenience, uncomfortable and frightening, even temporarily life threatening, but not disabling. The medical evidence demonstrates otherwise. Dr. Henry K. Mohler, in a standard medical textbook published in 1919, gives the following prognosis for this derangement of the body's normal response to heat.

> Although a patient may survive a severe attack of sunstroke, in a large percentage of cases the subject is never restored to his original health. Intolerance of heat, even a mild degree thereof, is a common after compliant.... Frequently various cerebral conditions are complained of, and physical disturbances, such as loss of memory, irritability, insomnia, mental hebetude [absence of mental alertness and affect], and dementia are not uncommon....

Furthermore, this reappraisal of Anse's health gives a reasonable explanation for the transformation of Anse Bundren from the shy, but hard-working, young man who cared enough about Addie to risk rejection of his courtship, into the indecisive, ineffectual and emotionally "dead" man of the novel's main action.

One can also find in this hypothesis a possible explanation for the inconsistencies and apparent hypocrisy of Anse's actions in regard to Addie's burial. The young and ambitious Anse, who was proud of having an honest name, would have shared the distaste of his class for being indebted to anyone else and would have been extremely reluctant to leave a promise unfulfilled. We see his spiritual survival in the Anse ... who desires to function but is unable to do so. This inability to function is another logical result of the heat stroke.

If Anse's personality did change as a result of the sunstroke the change could account for Addie's assertion that her husband is "dead." "He did not know that he was dead, then". This announcement comes after Addie's account of Darl's birth and would thus seem to indicate a change in Anse rather than an initial appraisal of his character. If Anse had always been "dead," why did it take so long for Addie to notice it? But the lack of affect or appropriate emotional response ... would be aptly termed a kind of death, especially by someone like Addie, who seems to crave a higher level of emotional intensity than more conventional people such as Cora Tull are able to envision. Anse's very condition of reduced mental abilities would preclude his understanding either the changes in himself or his wife's reaction to these changes....

Physical Effects of Toothlessness

Although anhidrosis and the other residual effects of heat stroke may be Anse's most serious health problems, they are not his only afflictions. Anse also suffers the ongoing problem of having had no teeth for fifteen years. However, pulling rotten teeth is not an uncomplicated solution to the problems they cause. In a culture without canned or pureed foods or nutritional supplements a person left without teeth will probably suffer from poor nutrition as well. Or as Anse puts it: "in fifteen years I aint et the victuals He aimed for man to eat to keep his strength up". To deny the literal meaning of Anse's toothlessness as an emblem of poverty is to deny the importance of socioeconomic setting for Faulkner's work.

A Crippling Accident and Poverty

The loss of his teeth is not the only other major health problem Anse has suffered. In Jewel's section we find a brief reference to Anse "laid sick with that load of wood fell on him". Since this accident to Anse is mentioned in the same sentence as Cash's crippling fall from the church roof, one may deduce

As I Lay Dying and Family Dysfunction

Leonardo da Vinci sketched this toothless profile, titled Caricature Head Study of an Old Man, in the early sixteenth century. Viewpoint author Rita Rippetoe discusses the symbolism of Anse's toothlessness. © Leonardo da Vinci/Bridgeman Art Library/Getty Images.

that it was fairly serious. If it involved broken bones, as seems likely, the period of convalescence could have been considerable....

Anse is not a well man by any reasonable standard. The chronic invalidism resulting from the after-effects of heat stroke, a possible temporarily incapacitating back injury, years without teeth, feet deformed by childhood poverty: these clearly mark him as a "misfortunate" man whose misfortunes explain his deficiencies of character, Anse is not a man one would wish for as a husband, father or neighbor, but he is neither the bundle of inexplicable contradictions described by Bleikasten nor the calculating villain condemned by Brooks. . . . Poverty and hard work have cruelly marked Anse's toothless mouth and his toenailess feet. But the most enduring of his afflictions is the anhidrosis, which ironically reveals itself by lack of a mark, the shirts left unstained by sweat, the anhidrosis which deprives him of the ability to earn his bread by the sweat of his brow, as his society tells him he is destined to do.

Jewel as Outsider and Man of Action

Peter G. Beidler

Peter G. Beidler, who specializes in medieval and American literature, is the Lucy G. Moses Distinguished Professor of English Emeritus at Lehigh University.

In the following selection Beidler describes Jewel, Addie's illegitimate son, as an especially complex character who is often described in the novel as wooden. Woodenness refers to his hardheartedness but also to his resolve in, for example, working hard for his horse. His character is also revealed in what he says, especially his impatience with indecision and inaction. His speech, full of swearing, suggests his intolerance with members of his family, perhaps even a loathing for them. When he swears, it is not in jest; he means it—an ironic stance for a preacher's son to take. More than others in the family he acts impulsively and illogically, as when he allows Anse to trick him into selling his beloved horse. By his refusal to join the family in the wagon, he flaunts his independence from and scorn for them. He is in sharp contrast to Darl, who is articulate and aware of his inner self.

Perhaps the most obvious of Faulkner's techniques of revealing Jewel is straight physical description. On the first page of the novel Darl gives us the first of several references to Jewel's woodenness: "Still staring straight ahead, his pale eyes like wood set into his wooden face, he crosses the floor in four strides with the rigid gravity of a cigar-store Indian dressed in patched overalls and endued with life from the hips

Peter G. Beidler, "Faulkner's Technique of Characterization," *Etudes Anglaises*, vol. 54 no. 3, Sept. 1968, pp. 236–242. Copyright © 1968 by Peter G. Beidler. All rights reserved. Reproduced by permission.

down". Jewel's woodenness is clearly important because Faulkner mentions it often, not only through Darl—"Jewel's eyes look like pale wood", he is "wooden-backed, wooden-faced, moving only from his hips down"—but also through such characters as Dewey Dell—"Jewel sits on his horse like they were both made out of wood".

Jewel's Talent and Hard-Heartedness

Jewel's woodenness is certainly meant to suggest that hard, inflexible purposefulness which permits him to earn the money for his horse, to rescue the coffin and tools from the river, and to save the coffin and livestock from the burning barn. It may also reflect a certain deadness in him, a hard-heartedness which permits him to commit Darl to an insane asylum and a hard-headedness which prevents him, as we shall soon see, from engaging in much verbal thinking. . . .

Jewel's Impatience with Inaction

Jewel does not say much in the novel, but much of what he says reveals, for example, his love and his need of action. He is always wanting to *do* something, and often becomes angrily impatient when the others show caution or want to stop for a moment. As they carry Addie's coffin from the house, Anse wants to stop and lock the door, but Jewel refuses to wait: "Come on," he says, "Come on". When Cash wants to stop and wait for more help because the coffin is not properly balanced, the impatient Jewel tells him, "Then turn loose", and charges on down the hill. When the three brothers finally discover just where the ford in the river is, Jewel says, "Well, goddamn it, lets get across, then". Darl and Cash pause to discuss what each of the three should do, but Jewel hurries them on: "I don't give a damn [what I do]. Just so we do something. Sitting here, not lifting a goddamn hand . . .".

What Jewel says, then, is revealing, but how he says it is just as revealing. It is impossible not to notice, for example, the extent to which Jewel uses swear-words. To be sure, almost all of the men in *As I Lay Dying* do some swearing, but it is pretty low-powered stuff and is hardly ever meant seriously. Anse's "Durn them boys" and Peabody's "I'll be damned if I can see why I don't quit" are typical of the swearing the other men occasionally engage in. Jewel, however, hardly ever opens his mouth without damning someone or something. In the few times that he speaks he uses "goddamn" twenty-four times, "damn" five times, and "hell" fifteen times. And he is not jesting or merely proving himself one of the boys when he swears; he means it when he says to Darl, "Goddamn you. Goddamn you." . . .

Jewel's Impulsiveness and Illogic

The fact that this preacher's son is so anxious to damn everyone and everything to hell—including his family and his horse—is important for other reasons than that it helps us to identify his speeches. It reinforces Jewel's tallness—"he is a head taller than any of the rest of us, always was"—and his general aloofness that he places himself far enough above others to damn them. Jewel's swearing also reveals him to be a man of quick-tempered impulsiveness. . . .

The mere fact that only one of the fifty-nine sections is told from Jewel's consciousness reinforces Jewel's inability to think verbally or logically. Faulkner gives us only one *Jewel* section, not because he wants to keep us at a distance from Jewel, but simply because there is very little that can be reported from Jewel's mind. . . .

It is important that Jewel is tall, for example, because the rest of the Bundren children are shorter. It is important that Jewel swears, because no one else in the novel swears as much, or in the same way. Certain character traits take on greater significance, or are thrown into greater relief, when they are compared with similar or different traits in other characters. If Jewel is a man of action rather than a man of thought, we are aware of this fact at least in part because his chief character foil, Darl, is very much a man of thought. That Darl is a thinking man is revealed not only by the sheer number (nineteen, or one-third of the total) and length (an average of three and a half pages) of the sections told through Darl's consciousness, but also by their style and subject matter, for Darl's musings, unlike Jewel's, are often poetic and philosophic. Then, too, whereas Jewel relies on swearing to express his feelings of antagonism toward Darl, Darl manages, through his greater command of words and rhetoric, to taunt Jewel much more effectively without swearing: "It's not your horse that's dead, Jewel"; "Your mother was a horse [whore?], but who was your father, Jewel?". Jewel's responses to these subtle but supremely effective taunts emphasize the difference between the two brothers. To the first he can reply only "Goddamn you. Goddamn you." In response to the second he says only, "You goddamn lying son of a bitch." . . .

Reports of Jewel's Family

Surely we must be wary of the reports of Jewel's own family, since family jealousies and prejudices will certainly come into play. Can we trust Dewey Dell when she says that "Jewel don't care about anything he is not kin to us in caring, not carekin"? Can we completely believe her when we know that Jewel does care enough about his kin to take more risks than anyone else to retrieve Cash's tools? Can we trust Anse when he says to Jewel that "You got no affection nor gentleness for her [Addie]. You never had"? Why should we when we see that Jewel risks his life to save her coffin from fire and flood, and that he gives up his precious horse so that Anse can get her buried in Jefferson?

Can we even trust Darl enough to accept his reporting of what Anse said? Anse's accusation that Jewel had "no affection nor gentleness" for his mother is reported—perhaps significantly—in one of Darl's sections, not one of Anse's. Is Darl simply reporting what *he* thinks, or what he *wants* Anse to think? There is no place in this study for a detailed analysis of Darl's character, but there is evidence that Darl is insanely jealous of Jewel because he, not Darl, received Addie's love. Darl therefore hates Jewel so thoroughly that he cannot be trusted *not* to distort—consciously or unconsciously—what he reports of him. Especially suspect are subjective judgments such as Darl's that Jewel is "like a little boy in the dark" flailing his courage "and suddenly aghast into silence by his own noise".

I am aware, of course, that by questioning the reliability of Darl's reporting I am casting doubt on a great deal of what we know, or think we know, about Jewel, because most of what we "know" about him we learn through Darl. My point is that the task of analyzing character becomes almost impossibly complex because we cannot fully trust anyone about anything. Before we can decide what characterizes a man, we must somehow sift out the true from the false in the shifting quicksand of opinions and "facts" we are given by different reporters at different times....

Jewel's Actions

We can be quite sure, ..., that Jewel does earn himself the money for that horse, and that he does later sacrifice the horse for his mother and the common family cause. And he does save his mother's coffin, almost single-handedly, from fire and flood. We can say, then, that Jewel has drive, determination, and concern for something besides himself. From here we can move up to less basic actions: Jewel's insistence on taking his horse on the journey, his continual insistence on action, while the others sit and talk, and his rejection, often rude, of all offers of assistance. These reveal him to be an individualist and a man of action. It is true that most of these actions are reported to us by characters who may not be entirely trustworthy, but we can probably assume that in basic matters of fact like these they would not deceive themselves or try to deceive others. Then, too, more than one character often attests to, or refers to, the same basic facts of action. It is largely in matters of interpretation, innuendo, and tone that we must be suspicious.

Vardaman's Reactions to Death Are Normal

Floyd C. Watkins and William Dillingham

Floyd C. Watkins and William Dillingham were both Distinguished Professors of English at Emory University. Watkins specialized in southern literature and Dillingham was the author of four books on Herman Melville.

Many critics interpret Vardaman (Addie's and Anse's youngest son), in two ways: as an idiot and as a mere symbol. In this excerpt, Watkins and Dillingham disagree with these views, arguing that Vardaman, who is probably no more than eight years old, reacts to his mother's death as any normal child might do. His lack of experience with death leaves him with no tools to handle the loss of the only person who seems to care for him. This leads him to confuse the two important events of his day—his catching and killing of the fish and the death of his mother. Her death is especially traumatizing since he has not accepted the seriousness of her illness and is stunned by seeing and hearing Cash nail her coffin shut.

A catalogue of the unusual and abnormal characters in William Faulkner's fiction would be shocking even to many scholars and especially to the large number of general readers who have tried to read Faulkner's works and found them obscure or perverted—or both. This list would certainly include Vardaman Bundren, the child in *As I Lay Dying*....

Vardaman as an Idiot

Certainly some of his actions and thoughts seem unusual. In what must be one of the shortest chapters in fiction, Vardaman says to himself simply but enigmatically, "My mother is a

Floyd C. Watkins and William Dillingham, "The Mind of Vardaman Bundren," *Philological Quarterly*, vol. 39, 1960, pp. 247–251. Copyright © 1960 by Philological Quarterly. All rights reserved. Reproduced by permission.

fish." And later he bores holes into his mother's coffin and on into her face in an attempt to give the corpse air to breathe.

These and other actions have caused Faulkner's critics to call Vardaman an idiot. Irving Howe, for example, argues that "Vardaman, pathetic and troubled, is locked in his idiocy," since he is "unable to distinguish between his dead mother and the fish he carries in his hand." ...

Vardaman as Symbolic

Critics who are not fully convinced that Vardaman is an idiot generally offer symbolic and surrealistic explanations of his confusion. Roma King, Jr., for example, gives him a little more intelligence by labeling him "the moronic child, [who] confuses his mother with the fish." ...

These two kinds of views of Vardaman present a dilemma: He is a poetic idiot, or he is so surrealistic and symbolic that he does not validly represent any natural level of human experience. But the dilemma is false. Though Vardaman may have several levels of symbolic meaning, he is not an idiot. Primarily he is an actual and not unintelligent child facing a real and human problem—the death of his mother. The problem is of such vast proportions that his past experiences do not enable him to interpret it or to cope with it emotionally.

A Young, Confused Child

The critics and scholars, first of all, have confused childhood with idiocy. That Vardaman is a young child is made clear. Although his age is never given in *As I Lay Dying*, Faulkner emphasizes his small size again and again. And from these various hints, it is hardly conceivable that he should be more than six to eight years old. The big fish he catches, according to Vernon Tull, is "durn nigh long as he is" and "durn nigh big as he is." After the death of Vardaman's mother, Cora Tull refers to him more than once as "the poor little tyke." And Peabody, the doctor, thinks "the durn little tyke is sitting on the top step, looking smaller than ever in the sulphur-coloured light." When Vardaman flees to the Tull house after Addie's death, he is hardly noticeable as he stands in the door: "I couldn't see nobody a-tall at first," Vernon relates, "until I looked down and around the door, lowering the lamp. He looked like a drowned puppy...." Physically as well as mentally, Vardaman is only a child. He is old enough to realize the presence of death but not old enough to comprehend it without profound shock and confusion.

The only seemingly idiotic thought in Vardaman's mind is his identification of his mother with the fish....

Shock of His Mother's Death

As Vardaman grows more and more aware of the presence of death, he brings closer and closer together two recent colossal events: the catching of the fish and the death of his mother. The fish is no more to Vardaman at first than a very proud catch which he wishes to show his mother. Then he is forced to kill it and cut it up, and immediately afterward he is taken to the bedside of his dying mother. Here he is abruptly initiated into the terrible but unmistakable truth of man's mortality. The realization that his mother is actually going to die has a pronounced influence on the boy, as Darl indicates in his description of the death scene. As Addie gives final instructions to Cash, Vardaman stares intensely at her, "his eyes round and his mouth beginning to open." His mental anguish is intensified when he actually witnesses his mother's death and when Dewey Dell falls hysterically across "the handful of rotten bones that Addie Bundren left." After the observant Darl describes Dewey Dell's reaction to Addie's death, he immediately notes its outward effect on Vardaman: "From behind pa's leg Vardaman peers, his mouth full open and all colour draining from his face into his mouth, as though he has by some means fleshed his own teeth in himself, sucking. He begins to move slowly backward from the bed, his eyes round, his pale face fading into the dusk like a piece of paper pasted on a failing wall, and so out of the door." There is nothing abnormal in this reaction for an emotional child, in a state of shock, and it is by no means an indication of inferior intelligence.

Grief and ignorance of death and the brief time interval between the death of the fish and that of his mother confuse Vardaman. Overwhelmed, he rushes from the side of his dead mother: "I run toward the back and come to the edge of the porch and stop. Then I begin to cry. I can feel where the fish was in the dust. It is cut up into pieces of not-fish now, not-blood on my hands and overalls. Then it wasn't so. It hadn't happened then." Here Faulkner indicates the child's failure to comprehend death by using the terms "not-fish" and "not-blood." He avoids the terms *dead* and *death*, just as Vardaman cannot comprehend the idea they express. Like the fish, Addie is "not flesh" and "not mother."

The Normalcy of Grief

For Vardaman, Addie's death has a sudden impact, and several events add to his perplexity. Previously he has not considered his mother seriously ill. As he searches desperately to place the blame for her death on someone, he naturally enough chooses the doctor, Peabody, who arrived at the Bundren home shortly before she died: "I can hear the bed and her face and them and I can feel the floor shake when he walks on it that came and did it. That came and did it when she was all right but he came and did it." Vardaman's mental strain increases when he learns that Cash is going to nail the lid on Addie's coffin. Unable to understand or accept his mother's death, he becomes more concerned and puzzled as he remembers a terrifying experience in his past. "I got shut up in the crib," he thinks, "the new door it was too heavy for me it went shut I couldn't breathe because the rat was breathing up all the air." Then little Vardaman smells his big fish, which Dewey Dell is frying on the wood stove. The climax is his notorious statement:

"My mother is a fish." But rather than the insane mumblings of an idiot boy, these words represent the impact of death on a young and normal mind. They are an analogy, a metaphor of death. The confusion comes only after a series of intensely painful events which initiate the little boy into the problems of mortality and manhood. To interpret him as an idiot is to ignore the primary and literal level of the novel.

That Vardaman's idiocy is the invention of the critics seems to be further verified by the attitudes of other characters toward the boy. Never is he referred to as an idiot. Characters aware of Darl's strangeness and insanity fail to note abnormality in Vardaman. . . .

Apparently considered normal for his age, Vardaman is sent upon errands and instructed to do odd jobs that would hardly be trusted to an idiot.

Vardaman's confusion thus is neither evidence that he is an idiot nor primarily recondite symbolism. . . . His words and acts are those of a sensitive child suffering bereavement.

Social Issues in Literature

CHAPTER 3

Contemporary Perspectives on Family Dysfunction

Child Neglect Is Prevalent but Not Widely Understood

Cailin O'Connor and Maggie McKenna

Cailin O'Connor is a consultant on family issues and writes the Research Review for the National Alliance of Children's Trust and Prevention Funds. Maggie McKenna is also a consultant on family and social programs and an associate clinical professor of public health at the University of Washington.

In the following essay, O'Connor and McKenna note that child neglect, which receives little attention, is the most prevalent form of mistreatment of children. Seventy-eight percent of maltreated children who came to the attention of Child Protective Services in 2010 were victims of neglect, they assert. Thirty-two percent of child fatalities in the same period were the result of neglect. Abuse in the form of neglect can often be kept "below the radar" where it is not easily detected. The most recognized form of neglect is physical, but an equally harmful form of neglect is emotional or psychological. The parents who emotionally neglect their children are typically depressed, disorganized, socially isolated, and addicted to drugs or alcohol, and majority of neglectful parents live in poverty.

The National Alliance of Children's Trust and Prevention Funds launched an initiative in 2011 to increase national focus on prevention of child neglect, with funding from the Doris Duke Charitable Foundation. As one of the first steps in that initiative, the Alliance conducted a preliminary review of the literature on child neglect. The following is a brief summary of the literature review so far, focusing on risk and pro-

Cailin O'Connor and Maggie McKenna, "Spotlight on Child Neglect," *Research Review*, vol. 2 no. 1, Winter 2010, pp. 1–7. www.ctfalliance.org/researchreview.htm. Copyright © 2010 by the National Alliance of Children's Trust and Prevention Funds. All rights reserved. Reproduced by permission.

tective factors for neglect. With more neglect-specific research focusing on risk factors than protective factors, the picture painted is not as strength-based as the Alliance would like it to be. Over the next three years, the Alliance intends to seek out and promote more research into protective factors and enhance our collective understanding of what we can do to ensure that families are able to meet their children's needs. That work will look at research, policies, programs, and practices that hold promise for the primary prevention of child neglect.

Extensiveness of Neglect

Neglect is less understood, yet more prevalent, than other forms of child maltreatment. For a variety of reasons, including lack of a clear and accepted definition, it has been less studied than physical, sexual, and emotional abuse. Notably, as rates of other forms of maltreatment appear to have decreased in recent years, rates of neglect have remained constant. Neglect is the most prevalent form of maltreatment reported to and confirmed by child protective services (CPS) agencies in America—often co-occurring with other forms of maltreatment. In 2010, 78% of child victims were neglected. Nearly one-third (32%) of child maltreatment fatalities in 2010 were attributed exclusively to neglect. In one study, families that were re-referred to CPS were referred for neglect more often than any other form of maltreatment, regardless of what form of maltreatment had been confirmed in their initial CPS contact. This pattern suggests that neglect may be occurring "below the radar" in many families before they come into contact with CPS, even as they are reported for other forms of maltreatment.

Emotional Neglect

Definitions and typologies of neglect vary, both among states and among researchers who study the phenomenon. Most definitions include the following types of neglect, grouped together in various ways: physical neglect, psychological or emotional neglect, educational neglect, supervisory neglect, medical neglect, and environmental neglect, which refers to serious hazards in the neighborhood or community that threaten a child's safety. [P.M.] Crittenden has proposed a typology focused on the mental processes of the neglecting parent: disorganized, emotionally neglecting, and depressed.

In addition to how they categorize types of neglect, definitions also vary in whether they emphasize a parent or caregiver's action or inaction, or the child's experience and unmet needs. For example, some parental actions may put a child at risk without any harm actually coming to the child—which would meet some, but not all, definitions of neglect. With a focus on the child's unmet needs, the threshold for neglectful behavior can vary greatly depending on the child's age and medical or mental health needs....

Finally, caregiving behavior can be said to fall on a spectrum. It is difficult to pinpoint exactly where on that spectrum sub-optimal parenting crosses over into neglect. Behaviors that have the potential to damage children's immediate or long-term well-being do not always reach the threshold for CPS intervention, particularly if they do not threaten the child's immediate physical safety. In many families, children's needs may go unmet and their physical and emotional well-being may be threatened due to neglectful behaviors that never come to the attention of CPS and would not be confirmed as neglect even if they were investigated. There is a great need for preventive services that target neglectful behaviors among families outside of CPS....

Characteristics of Neglectful Parents

Looking across three rigorous studies, [K.S.] Slack and colleagues identified a cluster of risk factors for child neglect at the level of parent characteristics. These factors, which were significant predictors of neglect in at least two of the three studies included in the analysis, include parental depression, substance abuse, health problems, social isolation, and high levels of parenting stress. Higher levels of maternal self-efficacy and involvement in child's activities emerged as protective factors that decreased the odds of neglect. Other studies have also identified maternal history of being neglected, young maternal age at first birth, low socioeconomic status, and limited maternal education as risk factors for neglect. Primary caregivers' mental health and substance abuse problems have also been found to be highly predictive of substantiated physical neglect.

Note that the majority of this research focuses on maternal characteristics. Very little research has focused on paternal characteristics related to maltreatment in general, and even less on neglect. One study did consider both parents' substance abuse and psychiatric disorders and their impact on child neglect. In the two-parent families studied, paternal substance abuse and psychopathology were related to paternal neglect of the child. However, mothers' psychopathology, particularly antisocial personality disorder, was more strongly correlated with fathers' neglect of children than was fathers' own psychopathology. There is a need for more research on the role of fathers in child neglect....

Research has also pointed to certain child characteristics that have been shown to influence the likelihood of neglect. Children who have greater needs—including those with medical problems and cognitive or developmental delays—are at heightened risk for neglect....

Poverty and Child Neglect

Family characteristics are also important determinants of child neglect. We categorize family economic circumstances here in the microsystem, although they could be construed as parental characteristics or reflections of community and neighborhood context. Slack and colleagues found that indicators of family poverty were strongly correlated with involvement in CPS for neglect, and correlated, though less strongly, with parents' self-report of neglectful behavior on the Conflict Tactics Scale. Indicators such as public benefit receipt, difficulty paying rent, unemployment, having utilities shut off, and inability to see a doctor due to cost were found to be related to neglect.

Another study ... found that perceived material hardship and infrequent employment were strongly associated with neglect, as were parenting characteristics including low parental warmth, use of physical discipline, and allowing frequent television viewing by the child. Parenting characteristics were not found to mediate the link between material hardship and neglect, although they did partially explain the link between employment and neglect.

However, a study of physical neglect in particular found that, while poverty was correlated with substantiated cases of physical neglect, other factors were more important. . . .

Once again, Crittenden brings another perspective. She argues that the relationship between poverty and neglect is not causal, but that something else—namely, distortions of mental processing—make some parents more likely both to live in poverty and to neglect their children. This theory also helps to explain those cases where we see intergenerational transmission of poverty and/or parenting styles, as children raised by parents with these distorted mental processes are likely to develop their own distorted mental processes.

Marriage May Not Be Essential for a Functional Family

Jessica Bennett and Jesse Ellison

Jessica Bennett and Jesse Ellison, editors and writers for Newsweek, *cover social and gender issues.*

In the following article, Bennett and Ellison note that many of the practical reasons for getting married are no longer operative for women. They say women no longer need to depend on a husband for a livelihood, noting that a majority of the workforce is now female and in two-thirds of American families, women are the chief breadwinners or co-breadwinners. Marriage itself, as an institution in the United States, appears to be in decline with Americans' having the highest divorce rate in the Western world. For these and other reasons, the authors point to more couples' choosing of cohabitation, successfully engaging in a long-term committed relationship without a legal document. The authors say that studies show these couples lose none of the benefits of married life and instead may be better parents, spending more time with their children.

Every year around this time [June], the envelopes begin to arrive. Embossed curlicues on thick-stock, cream-colored paper ask for "the pleasure of our company" at "the union of," "the celebration of," or "the wedding of." With every spring, our sighs get a little deeper as we anticipate another summer of rote ceremony, cocktail hour, and, finally, awkward dancing.

Jessica Bennett and Jesse Ellison, "I Don't: The Case Against Marriage," *Newsweek*, June 11, 2010. Copyright © 2010 The Newsweek/Daily Beast Company LLC. All rights reserved. Used by permission and protected by the Copyright Laws of the United States. The printing, copying, redistribution, or retransmission of the Material without express written permission is prohibited.

Sure, some weddings are fun, but too often they're a formulaic, overpriced, fraught rite of passage, marking entry into an institution that sociologists describe as "broken." . . .

Women's Status Change

Women now constitute a majority of the workforce; we're more educated, less religious, and living longer, with vacuum cleaners and washing machines to make domestic life easier. We're also the breadwinners (or co-breadwinners) in two thirds of American families. In 2010, we know most spousal rights can be easily established outside of the law, and that Americans are cohabiting, happily, in record numbers. We have our own health care and 401(k)s and no longer need a marriage license to visit our partners in the hospital. For many of us, marriage doesn't even mean a tax break.

The numbers are familiar but staggering: Americans have the highest divorce rate in the Western world. . . .

To tell you what you already know, the American family is in the throes of change. Gone are the days of the nuclear nest; in its wake is a motley mix of single parents, same-sex couples, and, yes, unmarried monogamists. Anthropologist Helen Fisher, who studies the nature of love, might say that's a symptom of our biology: she believes humans aren't meant to be together forever, but in short-term, monogamous relationships of three or four years. For us, it's not that we reject monogamy altogether—indeed, one of us is going on six years with a partner—but that the idea of marriage has become so tainted, and simultaneously so idealized, that we're hesitant to engage in it. Boomers may have been the first children of divorce, but ours is a generation for whom multiple households were the norm. We grew up shepherded between bedrooms, minivans, and dinner tables, with stepparents, half-siblings, and highly complicated holiday schedules. You can imagine, then—amid incessant high-profile adultery scandals—that we'd be somewhat cynical about the institution. (Till death do

A businesswoman carries a baby. Viewpoint authors Jessica Bennett and Jesse Ellison observe that women no longer have to get married to support a family. © Ariel Skelley/Blend Images/Getty Images.

us part, *really*?) "The question," says Andrew Cherlin, the author of *The Marriage-Go-Round*, "is not why fewer people are getting married, but why are so many still getting married?"

Apprehension About Marriage

The feminist argument against marriage has long been that it forces women to conform—as [feminist and activist] Gloria Steinem once put it, marriage is an arrangement "for one and a half people." No woman we know would date a man who'd force her into the kitchen—and even Steinem eventually got hitched—but we'd be fools to think we've completely shed the roles associated with "husband" and "wife." Men's contributions to housework and child rearing may have doubled since the 1960s, yet even among dual-earning couples, women still do about two thirds of the housework. (One study even claims that the simple act of getting married creates seven hours more housework for women each week.) In the workplace, meanwhile, women who use their partner's name are regarded as less intelligent, less competent, less ambitious, and thus less likely to be hired. We may date the most modern men in the world, but we've heard enough complaints to worry: if we tie the knot, does life suddenly become a maze of TV dinners, shoes up on the coffee table, and dirty dishes? "The bottom line is that men, not women, are much happier when they're married," says Philip Cohen, a sociologist at the University of North Carolina who studies marriage and family.

Since the early 1900s, the driving force behind marriage, along with procreation, was that women couldn't land well-paying jobs: we relied on our husbands to survive. As recently as 1967, two thirds of female college students (versus 5 percent of men) said they would marry somebody they didn't love if he met their other criteria—primarily, the ability to support them financially. But today, we no longer need to "marry up": women are more educated (we make up nearly 60 percent of college graduates) and better compensated (urban women in their 20s actually outearn their male peers). We are also the so-called entitled generation, brought up with lofty expectations of an egalitarian adulthood; told by helicopter parents and the media, from the moment we exited the womb, that we could be "whatever we wanted"—with infinite opportunities to accomplish those dreams. So you can imagine how, 25 years down the line, committing to another person—for life—would be nerve-racking. (How do you know you've found "the one" if you haven't vetted all the options?) "We've entered the age of last-minute tickets to Moscow, test-tube children, cross-continental cubicles and encouraged paternity leaves," write the authors of *The Choice Effect*, about love in an age of too many options. The result, they say, is "a generation that loves choice and hates choosing."

Love and High Expectations

Which means that when we do tie the knot, we do it for love. Young people today don't want their parents' marriage, says Tara Parker-Pope, the author of *For Better*—they want all-encompassing, head-over-heels fulfillment: a best friend, a business partner, somebody to share sex, love, and chores. In other words, a "soulmate"—which is what 94 percent of singles in their 20s describe what they look for in a partner. . . .

So while little girls may still dream of Prince Charming, they'll be more likely to keep him if they don't expect too much. Research shows that the more education and financial independence a woman has—in other words, the more success she has outside the home—the more likely she is to stay married. (In states where fewer wives have paid jobs, for example, divorce rates tend to be higher.) But when these egalitarian, independent couples decide not to marry at all, they lose none of that stability. Just take a look at couples in Europe: they're happier, less religious, and more likely to believe that marriage is an outdated institution, and their divorce rate is a fraction of our own. Not being married may make it slightly easier to walk away—at least legally—but if you've gone to the lengths to establish a life together, is it really all that different? Studies show that never-married couples with the intention of forever are just as likely to stay together as married ones. And for all the talk of marriage being good for families, a study of the Scandinavian countries—where a majority of children are born out of wedlock—found that kids actually spend more time with their parents than American children do. Work and living habits surely factor into that reality, but the point is this: what's good for children is stability. The decline of marriage "doesn't have to spell catastrophe," says Stephanie Coontz, the author of *Marriage, a History*. "We can make marriages better and make nonmarriages work as well."

Some Women Have No Instinct for Mothering

Mary Sojourner

Arizona-based Mary Sojourner is a writer, lecturer, and environmental activist who writes the She Bets Her Life *blog on Psychology Today's website.*

Surprisingly, many women who love their children hate being mothers. One contributing factor may be physical, that is, the number of specific brain neurons they have. The general, longstanding assumption is that all women, and especially those with children, have a natural instinct for mothering. But recent inquiries have shown that this is not necessarily true. Some women face a curious situation in that they adore their children but hate mothering. Writer Mary Sojourner encountered this personally in a writing class where several women expressed the same sentiment of hating to mother. The maternal instinct was simply not present. More and more women who have attended Sojourner's lectures around the country have expressed their shame at this deficiency. She found physiological evidence that the lack of instinct for mothering had to do with lack of mothering brain cells. The fewer of these particular neurons a woman has, the greater is her challenge to overcome her distaste for shouldering the heavy responsibilities that come with mothering.

The woman's voice was fragile. She looked up from her writing and said, "There's something wrong with me." We were in a writing circle with eight other women. The room was silent, even the whisper of pens on paper had stopped. "Can you tell us what's wrong?" I said.

Mary Sojourner, "She Bets Her Life," *Psychology Today*, May 23, 2010. Copyright © 2010 by Sussex Publishers, Inc. All rights reserved. Reproduced by permission.

The woman put down her notebook. "I think so," she said. "You said something at the beginning of this circle that has stayed with me. You said that you have never had any maternal instinct." I nodded, "That's true."

"But you gave birth to four children and raised three of them pretty much by yourself?"

"That's also true."

"And they turned out to be good people."

"Absolutely."

Unhappiness with Her Role

The woman put her hands over her face. Her voice was muffled. "I love my kids," she said, "but I hate being a mom." She looked up. Three other women in the circle nodded. "Three other women feel the same way," I said. "I think," the woman said quietly, "I'd like it if we wrote about this. And maybe read what we've written."

That was precisely what we did. At the circle's end, I watched quietly as we packed up our notebooks and pens. For the first time in my adult life, I didn't feel the thread of shame I've carried for so long. Each woman who had children had written of her delight, ambiguity and exhaustion in her work as a mother. One of the women who was not a mother wrote of her anger that she was defined as "not a mother"—by her family, her friends and the greater world. "What is the word," she wrote, "for a women who either cannot or chooses not to be a mother?"

From that time on I spoke openly about my lack of maternal instincts—when I taught writing circles, gave talks, sat on panels examining women and creativity. I was afraid each time. I felt as though I held out my hand with something as elemental and fragile as an Autumn leaf. No one ever attacked me for what I felt. After every class or event, one or more mothers (and grand-mothers) came up to me and spoke of their own fears or anger or shame. We often talked about our sense that we had worked especially hard at mothering, had trained ourselves to respond when we didn't want to respond, nurtured when the very cells in our bodies seemed to not know how to cuddle or cradle.

Gambling to Escape Caregiving

I read from *She Bets Her Life* last Thursday [May 2010], at Sundance Books in Reno, Nevada. A young woman came up at the end of the reading and said, "I'm so glad you talked about why women gamble—especially when you said that most women don't go to casinos to socialize. I go to get away from taking care of everybody. I have three little kids and my husband's mom. It's my escape." I told her that nearly all the women I had met in casinos and gambling 12-step meetings had said the same thing. "It's been spun by the media into a demonic stereotype—you know, *Mom leaves kids in car outside casino while she gambles!*" "I would never do that," the woman said. "But, I've too often left them with my husband and not gotten home till morning. I know I have to stop. I hope I can find the courage to get some help."

Physical Causes

I googled "young mothers overwhelmed by mothering" before I began to write this post. I found dozens of sites. And I found yet again the evidence that the wiring in our brains can rule. *According to scientists at Richmond University in Virginia, women develop a set of "maternal neurons" that operate like "bad mother/good mother" switches in the brain. Using brain-scanning techniques, they have identified a cluster of brain cells, created during pregnancy and "switched on" after birth, that appear to correlate with good or bad parenting behaviours.*

"*We believe that a certain number of these 'maternal neurons' need to be 'switched on' for good mothering to take place,*" *explains Professor Craig Kinsley, whose research has so far been limited to rodents and small mammals. "Our research* showed that the mothers with fewer than this number of 'maternal neurons' tended to neglect or abuse their offspring, while those animals with the lowest numbers actually savaged or killed their own young."

Similar techniques could soon be used to identify human mothers with the capacity to abuse their children. A team at Yale University is already using brain scans to study the areas of the brain that drive good and bad mothering: "We have identified certain areas of the brain where there is a correlation between the level of neuron activity and measures of 'adequate' and 'inadequate' parenting," says Professor James Swain . . .

. . . Sian Busby believes that such measures could create a self-fulfilling prophecy. "My own experience has taught me how damaging a sense of innate culpability can be. Because I thought I had inherited the capacity to be a cruel mother, I became consumed by fear that I might do something to my baby. The notion that it was somehow out of my control was terrifying and unhelpful. Moreover, it prevented me from seeking the support I needed."

Professor Alison Fleming, director of the Centre for the Study of the Psychobiology of Maternal Behaviour at the University of Toronto. . . .is also concerned that the new research into maternal neurons could be used to argue diminished responsibility for those who abuse their children: "It's perfectly possible to be a good mother with 'bad genes'—or 'bad brain cells' for that matter—just as it is possible to be neglectful, abusive or inadequate with good ones."

Professor Kinsley disagrees: "We are all a slave to our brain function. An abusive mother has something malfunctioning in the brain so, in that respect, her behaviour is beyond her control." When it comes to studying the brain, questions of "bad" and "good" need to be replaced with notions of "broken" and "fixed", says Kinsley. "But it's not a question of whether we excuse a certain behaviour. The aim of our research is to identify brain malfunctions so we can work towards fixing them."

But is it possible to fix or rewire a brain? "Of course it is," says Kinsley. "Just because a certain pattern of behaviour has a neuro-anatomical determinant does not mean that it is not possible to alter it. The brain is incredibly 'plastic', constantly responding to the environment and capable of incredible change." According to Kinsley, new mothers whose brain scans identified them as having inadequate numbers of maternal neurons could be targeted with counselling or nurse visiting programmes. "Such interventions would help to kickstart more maternal neurons, switching on circuits in the brain responsible for healthy, sensitive parenting behaviour."—Times Online, U.K.

Learning How to Mother

I remember women telling me that when they recognized that they didn't have the instinct for mothering, they knew they had to teach themselves how to care for their babies. I heard them speak of the difficult and courageous work they did to learn to cradle, to cuddle, to sit on the floor with their toddlers and play choo choo. Not all of us found a new motherly warmth beginning to flow through our bodies. But we continued to practice what we knew was critical for the well-being of our children.

I'm grateful that I raised my children in the Sixties and Seventies. Women were challenging the old definitions of who we are. It was a time when I could share how I felt with other women—in consciousness-raising groups, in friendships, in my therapy group. I didn't feel quite so alone with my secret. Despite that, the shame of "having the maternal instinct of a male mink" haunted me till I looked at the faces of the women in my writing circle and saw that I was not alone. None of the friends of my young womanhood felt the way I did. They listened. They did not judge. But there was no way for them to understand.

I offer this piece to any of you who have been baffled and pained by what you feel as you mother. I offer it to my dear friend, Viviane, who fought through stunning post-partum depression. I offer it to the spirit of my mother, who held my hand as she lay dying and said, "My one regret is that the god-damned depression robbed me of being able to be the mother I longed to be." And I offer it with love to my adult children—they know why.

Fathers Are Important in the Healthy Development of Children

Jeffrey Rosenberg and W. Bradford Wilcox

Jeffrey Rosenberg is the founder of Rosenberg Communications, which was hired by the National Fatherhood Initiative to design and implement media to educate the public about the issue of absentee fatherhood. Rosenberg was previously the communications director for the US Department of Health and Human Services. W. Bradford Wilcox is assistant professor of sociology at the University of Virginia and a member of the James Madison Society at Princeton University. His research focuses on religion, fatherhood, marriage, and parenting.

In the following report, Rosenberg and Wilcox relate the importance of fathers in the healthy development of children. They point to a connection between involvement of fathers and outcomes in several key areas, including education and social wellbeing. The authors report that fathers can influence children through direct and indirect relationships, such as that between the child's father and mother. Children with positive relationships with their fathers were at less risk for certain behaviors such as lying and demonstrated better overall physical and emotional health.

A noted sociologist, Dr. David Popenoe, is one of the pioneers of the relatively young field of research into fathers and fatherhood. "Fathers are far more than just 'second adults'

Jeffrey Rosenberg and W. Bradford Wilcox, "Fathers and Their Impact on Children's Well-Being," *The Importance of Fathers in the Healthy Development of Children*, US Department of Health and Human Services: Administration for Children and Families, 2006, pp. 11–13.

in the home," he says. "Involved fathers bring positive benefits to their children that no other person is as likely to bring." Fathers have a direct impact on the well-being of their children....

This [report] lays out the connection between fathers and child outcomes, including cognitive ability, educational achievement, psychological well-being, and social behavior. The [report] also underscores the impact of the father and mother's relationship on the well-being of their children. While serving as an introduction to the issues, this [report] is not intended as an exhaustive review of the literature. For the reader wishing to learn more, the U.S. Department of Health and Human Services, the National Fatherhood Initiative, and the National Center for Fathering are valuable resources.

The Mother-Father Relationship

One of the most important influences a father can have on his child is indirect—fathers influence their children in large part through the quality of their relationship with the mother of their children. A father who has a good relationship with the mother of their children is more likely to be involved and to spend time with their children and to have children who are psychologically and emotionally healthier. Similarly, a mother who feels affirmed by her children's father and who enjoys the benefits of a happy relationship is more likely to be a better mother. Indeed, the quality of the relationship affects the parenting behavior of both parents. They are more responsive, affectionate, and confident with their infants; more self-controlled in dealing with defiant toddlers; and better confidants for teenagers seeking advice and emotional support.

One of the most important benefits of a positive relationship between mother and father ... is the behavior it models for children. Fathers who treat the mothers of their children with respect and deal with conflict within the relationship in an adult and appropriate manner are more likely to have boys who understand how they are to treat women and who are less likely to act in an aggressive fashion toward females. Girls with involved, respectful fathers see how they should expect men to treat them and are less likely to become involved in violent or unhealthy relationships. In contrast, research has shown that husbands who display anger, show contempt for, or who stonewall their wives (i.e., "the silent treatment") are more likely to have children who are anxious, withdrawn, or antisocial.

Educational Achievement

Children with involved, caring fathers have better educational outcomes. A number of studies suggest that fathers who are involved, nurturing, and playful with their infants have children with higher IQs, as well as better linguistic and cognitive capacities. Toddlers with involved fathers go on to start school with higher levels of academic readiness. They are more patient and can handle the stresses and frustrations associated with schooling more readily than children with less involved fathers.

The influence of a father's involvement on academic achievement extends into adolescence and young adulthood. Numerous studies find that an active and nurturing style of fathering is associated with better verbal skills, intellectual functioning, and academic achievement among adolescents. For instance, a 2001 U.S. Department of Education study found that highly involved biological fathers had children who were 43 percent more likely than other children to earn [more] and 33 percent less likely than other children to repeat a grade.

Marriage and Fatherhood

Caring, involved fathers exist outside of marriage. They are more likely, however, to be found in the context of marriage. There are numerous reasons for this, not the least of which

A father plays with his son, an activity that has a significant, positive impact on a child's development, according to Jeffrey Rosenberg and W. Bradford Wilcox. © Blend Images/Corbis.

being the legal and social norms associated with marriage that connect a father to the family unit. That may also explain, in part, why research consistently shows that the married mother-and-father family is a better environment for raising children than the cohabitating (living together) mother-and-father family.

It is interesting to note that, contrary to stereotypes about low-income, unmarried parents, a significant majority—more than 8 in 10—of urban, low-income fathers and mothers are in a romantic relationship when their children are born. Most of these couples expect that they will get married. One study found that more than 80 percent expected they would get married or live together. However, only 11 percent of these couples had actually married a year later. Why they do not marry is an interesting question open to conjecture. However, as Dr. Wade Horn, Assistant Secretary for Children and Families at the U.S. Department of Health and Human Services has pointed out, it may be because these couples receive very little encouragement to marry from the health and social services professionals with whom they come in contact.

Psychosocial Development

Even from birth, children who have an involved father are more likely to be emotionally secure, be confident to explore their surroundings, and, as they grow older, have better social connections with peers. These children also are less likely to get in trouble at home, school, or in the neighborhood. Infants who receive high levels of affection from their fathers (e.g., babies whose fathers respond quickly to their cries and who play together) are more securely attached; that is, they can explore their environment comfortably when a parent is nearby and can readily accept comfort from their parent after a brief separation. A number of studies suggest they also are more sociable and popular with other children throughout early childhood.

The way fathers play with their children also has an important impact on a child's emotional and social development. Fathers spend a much higher percentage of their one-on-one interaction with infants and preschoolers in stimulating, playful activity than do mothers. From these interactions, children learn how to regulate their feelings and behavior. Roughhousing with dad, for example, can teach children how to deal with aggressive impulses and physical contact without losing control of their emotions. Generally speaking, fathers also tend to promote independence and an orientation to the outside world. Fathers often push achievement while mothers stress nurturing, both of which are important to healthy development. As a result, children who grow up with involved fathers are more comfortable exploring the world around them and more likely to exhibit self-control and pro-social behavior.

One study of school-aged children found that children with good relationships with their fathers were less likely to experience depression, to exhibit disruptive behavior, or to lie and were more likely to exhibit pro-social behavior. This same study found that boys with involved fathers had fewer school behavior problems and that girls had stronger self-esteem. In addition, numerous studies have found that children who live with their fathers are more likely to have good physical and emotional health, to achieve academically, and to avoid drugs, violence, and delinquent behavior.

In short, fathers have a powerful and positive impact upon the development and health of children.

Mom's Favoritism Can Affect Kids, Sibling Rivalry as Adults

Sharon Jayson

Sharon Jayson has covered behavior and relationships for USA Today *since 2005.*

In the following article, Jayson reports on the impact of maternal favoritism on children and adults. She says that favoritism, while natural, can create problems in children and some long-lasting effects, such as increased sibling rivalry in adults. Jayson points to studies that show individual temperament can influence maternal favoritism, but she also notes that some researchers believe sibling jealousy to be a cultural phenomenon, particularly related to the "culture of individualism" in the United States. Experts suggest a variety of methods to combat feelings of jealousy, including explaining different treatment and allowing all children to get to be favored at different times.

There's no denying it. In any household with more than one child, kids seem to naturally compete for their mother's love and attention. And mothers swear they love every child equally.

But just maybe Mom does really love you best. Or is it just wishful thinking that you're her favorite?

"Mothers worry about that issue of 'Am I closer to one than I am to the other?'" says Cate Dooley, a psychologist with the Wellesley Centers for Women in Wellesley, Mass. "Mothers really need to let themselves off the hook. You're going to have different relationships with each child. It's OK."

Sharon Jayson, "Mom's Favoritism Can Affect Kids, Sibling Rivalries as Adults," *USA Today*, May 5, 2010. Copyright © 2010 Gannett. All rights reserved. Used by permission and protected by the Copyright Laws of the United States. The printing, copying, redistribution, or retransmission of the Material without express written permission is prohibited.

With Mother's Day around the corner [May 2010], new research is shedding some light on what happens when a parent—particularly the mother—gives more time or attention or privileges to one of the children. Past studies have found that less-favored siblings may suffer emotionally, with decreased self-esteem and behavioral problems in childhood, while adult children who were even slightly favored report higher well-being.

It could be a result of gender (favoring the same-sex or opposite-sex child), birth order (the oldest or the baby) or how easy or difficult a child's temperament may be, but a parent's differential treatment—real or perceived—has far-reaching effects, including fueling sibling rivalry, experts say. Such questions are particularly important for Baby Boomers; these unresolved feelings are playing out now in the care of aging parents. Experts agree the feeling that Mom always liked a sibling better can affect lifelong psychological well-being.

"Ask any family and they'll tell you who was the favorite one," says Jacqueline Plumez, a psychologist in Larchmont, N.Y. "People are very shaped by their family situations and how they were treated. You can be 80 years old and still hurt by it and the parent is long, long dead."

In her new book, *Mom Still Likes You Best*, author Jane Isay of New York City says favoritism is a "recipe for the next generation to not like each other."

Author Laurel Kennedy's new book, *The Daughter Trap*, devotes a chapter to sibling problems related to caregiving for aging parents. Kennedy, founder of a Chicago consulting firm for Baby Boomers called Age Lessons, interviewed 216 women and found that even though none of her questions asked directly about a parent favoring one child over another, about two-thirds of the women said there was a favored child, and most said it was "mother-focused."

"Out of the blue they'd say, 'She always liked my brother better, and he got to go to summer camp in 1968 and I didn't,'" Kennedy says.

Experts say it's not realistic to say everyone should be treated equally, because no two people are the same and they relate differently to others.

"It does not mean the parent loves or likes one child more. It has to do with who each of them is separately," says clinical psychologist Laurie Kramer of the University of Illinois at Urbana-Champaign.

Plumez, who interviewed adoptive parents and parents of biological children for an adoption book in 1982, found that "what matters most is whether your temperaments are simpatico."

"In some cases, parents would say they felt closer to their adopted kid or their biological kid," she says. "Two people who want to be in control are always going to be butting heads. Two people who are shy and withdrawn might get along well, unless the shy parent doesn't like that aspect of themselves and they try to push the naturally introverted child to be more extroverted."

Jodie Casagrande, 38, of Jamaica Plain, Mass., the mother of three sons, Lucca, 6; Matteo, who turns 4 next month, and Roman, 18 months, says her middle son is most like her.

"His personality is just like mine and we're always butting heads," she says.

Although her trio is showing some signs of sibling rivalry, she says, "it's not like it's all the time. I just noticed each of them getting jealous if I'm giving one of them attention in front of the other. I'll be sitting in the playroom and Roman will sit on my lap, then Matteo will want to sit on me and Lucca will fold his arms in and pout."

Kramer says it "seems as though most children are basically preprogrammed to watch how they're being treated in relation to their siblings."

Family Dysfunction in William Faulkner's As I Lay Dying

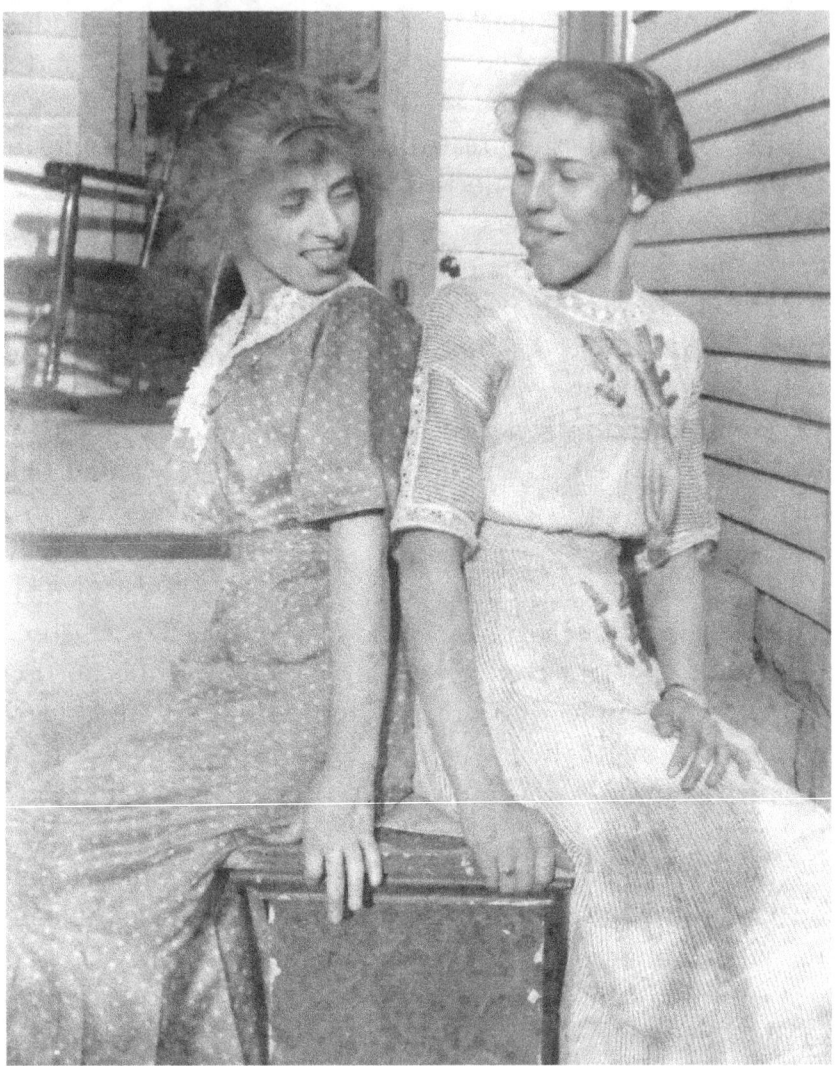

Sisters sit back-to-back and stick their tongues out at each other in this early-twentieth-century photograph. Reviewer Sharon Jayson examines the damage caused by maternal favoritism and sibling rivalry, which poisons the relationships in As I Lay Dying. *© DaZo Vintage Stock Photos/Images.com/Corbis.*

Culture or Instinct?

Mark Feinberg, a senior research associate at Pennsylvania State University in University Park, says this sensitivity may not be instinctual, however.

"I don't think we have an ingrained, hard-wired sibling jealousy part of our brain, but I think we're highly sensitive to fairness in social situations, and the family is the basic social situation for many years of our formative development," he says.

Another Penn State researcher, Susan McHale, who directs the Family Relationships Project, studied immigrant Mexican-American families. She didn't find a link between favoritism and problems in youth adjustment or parent-child relationships, suggesting that sibling rivalry is very "culture bound" and more related to a culture of individualism in the USA than the Mexican-American culture, which is more "communally oriented."

And McHale says favoritism is less an issue in larger families, where there's a coalition of siblings rather than an alliance between parent and offspring.

Mother of 10 Brenda O'Shea of Munster, Ind., says those family formations are at work in her own household. Her children—six boys and four girls—range in age from 22 months to 27 years.

"We try very consciously not to compare grades, abilities, talents, any of that sort of thing. We don't encourage competition between the kids," she says. "We find they encourage each other."

O'Shea, 49, a psychiatrist who stopped practicing 16 years ago to stay home with the kids, is attuned to emotional health.

"Families don't tend to talk about these issues. They don't explain it and kids are left to their own imagination," Kramer says. "'I'm not as good as my brother. She likes my sister better.'"

Her research has found that when parents explain why there may be some different treatment of a sibling and when the child considers it fair, there aren't any damaging consequences for the kids or their relationships with parents or siblings.

"Kids analyze these situations and say 'Is it because he's older or because I'm a girl or because moms always treat the older ones better or because they spend more time together or because my sister is very lonely and needs more attention?'" she says.

Being the favored one may also be problematic. Not-yet-published research co-written by Jennifer Jenkins, a professor of human development at the University of Toronto in Canada, shows being highly favored in a family may be as damaging to the child as being disfavored; both contribute to an increased chance of being aggressive. Jenkins says the findings are "explained either by children feeling bad about what seems to be unequal resource allocation in the family or adverse consequences on the sibling relationships."

Another new study she co-wrote has also found higher levels of differential parenting among more socioeconomically disadvantaged parents.

Earlier research co-written by Kramer and published in 1995 found that women who reported negative sibling relationships during childhood appear to have kids with more positive sibling relationships.

"Mothers realized they had experienced things with their parents that were not conducive to good sibling relationships and worked hard to not carry that through with their own kids," she says.

"Oftentimes, when they complain that way, a parent is likely to be a little bit defensive and say 'No, I don't' or 'I love you all the same.' Those answers are never very satisfying to young children," Kramer says. "It's important for parents to listen and try to put their defensiveness away."

Swapping Favorites

Ellen Weber Libby, a psychotherapist in Washington, D.C., and author of the book *The Favorite Child*, published this year [2010], says it's important that "the position of favoring gets rotated so every child grows up having experienced favoritism."

And parents should mix it up with the kids so that one parent isn't always with the same child and the other parent with the other child. The same goes for twins, she says.

Mother of three Sue Wilson, 56, of Stillwater, Minn., says she avoided favoritism when her oldest two were preschoolers by starting what she called "Child of the Day." That day's special child would have the favored spot, but the next day the other would. With the third, it became every three days. Her children, now 29, 27 and 24, rotated the benefits (such as who sat shotgun in the car, who got an extra cookie or any other special privilege that day) well into high school. "It stopped every argument," says Wilson. "I'd just say 'Who's Child of the Day?'"

And Wilson says her daughter wasn't automatically the favorite because she was the only girl.

But in other families, such as Libby's, there were clear favorites.

"I was always very aware that my brother was our mother's favorite and I was my father's favorite," she says.

Libby says children just want to know they are loved. But she says most people do want to have the "feeling that Mom loved me just a little bit more than everyone else."

"That's why so much gets focused on moms," she says.

For Further Discussion

1. In what ways might William Faulkner's life resonate in *As I Lay Dying*? See Wagner-Martin, Blotner, and Wittenberg.
2. Describe "motherhood" as it is presented in the novel. See Bassett, Kincaid, Hewson, and Wood.
3. Characterize Anse. What are his motives for his actions and what do they say about his character? See Faulkner, Rossky, and Rippetoe.
4. List the ways in which the family members disintegrate after Addie's death. Is her physical decay a symbol of that disintegration? Explain. See Beidler, Watkins and Dillingham, Bassett, and Rossky.
5. Discuss sibling relationships in the novel. In your judgment is there any enduring close connection between any of the siblings? Explain. See Bassett, Beidler, and Watkins and Dillingham.
6. What constitutes dysfunctional families today that parallel *As I Lay Dying*? See O'Connor and McKenna, and Bennett and Ellison.

For Further Reading

Erskine Caldwell, *Tobacco Road*, 1932.

William Faulkner, *The Sound and the Fury*, 1929.

William Faulkner, *Light in August*, 1932.

William Faulkner, *Absalom, Absalom!*, 1936.

William Faulkner, *Go Down, Moses and Other Stories*, 1942.

William Faulkner, *Snopes: A Trilogy*, 1964.

Carson McCullers, *The Member of the Wedding*, 1946.

Flannery O'Connor, *The Complete Stories*, 1971.

John Steinbeck, *The Grapes of Wrath*, 1939.

Eudora Welty, *The Collected Stories of Eudora Welty*, 1980.

Bibliography

Books

Andre Bleikasten — *As I Lay Dying.* Trans. Roger Little. Bloomington: Indiana University Press, 1973.

Cleanth Brooks — *William Faulkner: First Encounters.* New Haven, CT: Yale University Press, 1983.

Nancy Chodorow — *The Reproduction of Mothering.* Berkeley: University of California Press, 1978.

Malcolm Cowley — *The Faulkner-Cowley File: Letters and Memories 1944–1962.* New York: Viking, 1966.

Jane Greer — *Adult Sibling Rivalry: Understanding the Legacy of Childhood.* New York: Fawcett Books, 1993.

Irving Howe — *William Faulkner: A Critical Study.* New York: Vintage Books, 1952.

Frederick Karl — *William Faulkner: American Writer.* New York: Weidenfeld and Nicolson, 1989.

Martin Kreiswirth — *Figures of Division: William Faulkner's Major Novels.* New York: Methuen, 1986.

Annette Lareau	*Unequal Childhoods: Class, Race, and Family Life.* Berkeley: University of California Press, 2003.
Irving Malin	*William Faulkner. An Interpretation.* Stanford, CA: Stanford University Press, 1857.
Michael Millgate	*The Achievement of William Faulkner.* New York: Vintage Books, 1963.
David Minter	*William Faulkner: His Life and Work.* Baltimore: Johns Hopkins University Press, 1980.
Stephen M. Ross	"Shapes of Time and Consciousness in *As I Lay Dying*," in *William Faulkner's "As I Lay Dying": A Critical Casebook.* Ed. Dianne Cox. New York: Garland, 1985.
James Snead	*Figures of Division: William Faulkner's Major Novels.* New York: Methuen, 1986.
Eric J. Sundquist	*Faulkner: The House Divided.* Baltimore: Johns Hopkins University Press, 1983.
David Williams	*Faulkner's Women: The Myth and the Muse.* Montreal: McGill-Queens University Press, 1977.
Joel Williamson	*William Faulkner and Southern History.* New York: Oxford University Press, 1993.

Karl F. Zender — *The Crossing of the Ways: William Faulkner, the South, and the Modern World.* New Brunswick, NJ: Rutgers University Press, 1989.

Periodicals and Internet Sources

T.H. Adamowski — "'Meet Mrs. Bundren': *As I Lay Dying*—Gentility, Tact and Psychoanalysis," *University of Toronto Quarterly*, Spring 1980.

Calvin Bedient — "Pride and Nakedness: *As I Lay Dying*," *Modern Language Quarterly*, vol. 29, 1968.

Sheryl A. Benton — "Dysfunctional Families: Recognizing and Overcoming Their Effects," *Counseling Services of Kansas State University*, 1993. www.k-state.edu.

Frank Bruni — "The Enigma Beside Edwards," *New York Times*, June 5, 2012.

Reuben J. Ellis — "Faulkner's Totemism: Vardaman's 'Fish Assertion' and the Language Issue in *As I Lay Dying*," *Modern Fiction Studies*, Summer 1967.

Rosemary Franklin — "Animal Magnetism in *As I Lay Dying*," *American Quarterly*, Spring 1966.

Jack Gordon Goellner — "A Closer Look at *As I Lay Dying*," *Perspective*, Spring 1954.

Robert J. Kloss — "Faulkner's *As I Lay Dying*," *American Imago*, vol. 38, 1981.

Dayton Kohler	"William Faulkner and His Social Conscience," *College English*, December 1949.
M.M. Martin, C.M. Anderson, and K.A. Rocca	"Perceptions of the Adult Sibling Relationship," *North American Journal of Psychology*, March 1, 2005.
James M. Mellard	"Faulkner's Philosophical Novel: Ontological Themes in *As I Lay Dying*," *Personalist*, vol. 48, 1967.
Robert Nadeau	"The Morality of Act: A Study of Time," *Mosaic*, vol. 6, 1973.
Alan D. Perles	"*As I Lay Dying* as a Study of Time," *South Dakota Review*, vol. 10, 1972.
Constance Pierce	"Being, Knowing, and Saying in the 'Addie' Section of Faulkner's *As I Lay Dying*," *Twentieth Century Literature*, vol. 26, no. 3, 1980.
Karen R. Sass	"At a Loss for Words: Addie and Language in *As I Lay Dying*," *Faulkner Journal*, vol. 6, 1991.
Kenneth B. Sawyer	"The Hero in *As I Lay Dying*," *Faulkner Studies*, Spring–Summer 1954.
C. Stewart	"Parental Psychopathology and Paternal Child Neglect in Late Childhood," *Journal of Child and Family Studies*, vol. 15, no. 5, 2006.

John Tucker "Faulkner's *As I Lay Dying*: Working Out the Cubistic Bugs," *Texas Studies in Language and Literature*, Winter 1984.

Jan Viscomi "Natural Rhythms and Rebellion: Anse's Role in *As I Lay Dying*," *Modern Fiction Studies*, vol. 24, 1978.

Index

A

Academic achievement, role of fathers in, 125
Addie Bundren (*As I Lay Dying*)
  alienation felt by, 82–84
  body of, 86, 87
  burial of, 73–74, 84–85, 91
  centrality of, to novel, 20, 21, 52–53, 55–56, 71–80
  character of, 23
  Darl and, 61, 79–80, 87
  death of, 21, 54, 57, 75, 103–104
  Dewey Dell and, 53, 57–58, 86–87
  as earth-mother, 79–80
  female identity of, 82–83
  flaws of, 56
  Jewel and, 66, 77–78, 84
  marriage of, 47–48, 65–66, 72–73, 83
  motherhood and, 47–48, 75–76, 81–84
  rebellion by, 81–87
  religion and, 63–64
  sexuality of, 65–67, 81–83, 86, 87
  significance of name of, 68
  teaching career of, 10–11, 75, 82–83
Afterlife, 63–64, 82
Agamemnon, 9
American Academy of Arts and Letters, 25
Anhidrosis, 90–91, 94
Anse Bundren (*As I Lay Dying*)
  character of, 20–21, 56–57, 88–94
  cluelessness of, 53–54
  inaction of, 73, 74
  laziness of, 89, 90
  marriage of, 47–48, 65–66, 72–73, 83
  physical ailments of, 89–94
  reaction to death by, 51–52
  socioeconomic status of, 11
  sweatlessness of, 90–91, 94
  toothlessness of, 70, 89, 92, 94
As I Lay Dying (Faulkner)
  characters in, 21, 23, 49–54
  comic elements in, 54
  family dysfunction in, 10, 49–54
  focus of, 21
  historical context of, 10
  maternal influence in, 71–80
  mother-child relationships in, 52–53, 56, 59, 60–61, 71–80, 83–84, 86–87
  rebellion in, 81–87
  religious suppression in, 62–70
  sibling relationships in, 45–47, 57–58, 60–61, 98–99
  villain in, 45
  women in, 23, 65–70
  writing of, 19–21

B

Bailey, Julia, 27
Barnett, Ned, 29–30
Bassett, John Earl, 55–61
The Bear (Faulkner), 37

Beidler, Peter G., 95–100
Bennett, Jessica, 112–116
The Birth of Tragedy (Nietzsche), 63
Bleikasten, Andre, 89
Blotner, Joseph, 26–32
Body-loathing, 64–65
Brooks, Cleanth, 88–89
Bruni, Frank, 9
Bryant, Sally Bailey, 27
Bryant, Will, 27
Bundren family (*As I Lay Dying*)
    ancestry of, 10–11
    conflict in, 55–61
    Faulkner's view of, 42–48
    hardships encountered by, 49–54
    socioeconomic status of, 11
    See also specific characters
Busby, Sian, 120
Butler, Lelia, 35–36, 39

C

Cain and Abel, 9
Callie, Mammy, 30
Casagrande, Jodie, 131
Cash (*As I Lay Dying*), 21, 52, 54, 56, 60–61
Cherlin, Andrew, 114
Child neglect, 107–111
Child protective services (CPS), 108
Children
    parental favoritism and, 129–135
    relationships between mothers and, 52–53, 56, 59–61, 71–80, 83–87, 129–135
    role of fathers in development of, 123–128

Christianity, 63, 82
Civil War, 10
Clarke, Deborah, 87
Cohabitation, 113, 116, 127
Cohen, Philip, 115
Coontz, Stephanie, 116
Cora Tull (*As I Lay Dying*), 55–56, 69, 83, 92, 102
Cosmic absurdity, 53
Cowley, Malcolm, 25
Cows, symbolism of, 64–65, 67, *68*
Crichton, Kyle, 32

D

Darl (*As I Lay Dying*)
    Addie and, 61, 79–80, 87
    birth of, 75
    Cash and, 52, 61
    character of, 21, 59–60
    connection of, to earth, 80
    Dewey and, 45–47, 57–58
    insanity of, 43–44, 47, 50–51
    Jewel and, 98–99
    temperament of, 79
    as thoughtful man, 98
Death, 51–52, 64, 74–75, 103–104
Deception, 84
Dewey Dell (*As I Lay Dying*)
    Addie and, 53, 57–58, 86–87
    character of, 52, 54, 57–58
    conflict between brothers and, 21, 45–47, 57–58
    crop picking by, 11
    Darl and, 45–47, 57–58
    feeding family as responsibility of, 69–70
    motherhood for, 86–87
    pregnancy of, 57–58, 86–87
    sexuality of, 67, 69
    significance of name of, 69

Index

Dillingham, William, 101–105
Divorce, 113, 116
Doc Peabody (*As I Lay Dying*), 58, 102–103
Doctorow, E. L., 10
Doherty, Meta, 24
Dooley, Cate, 129
Dreiser, Theodore, 20
Dysfunctional family. *See* Family dysfunction

E

Edwards, Elizabeth, 9
Edwards, John, 9
Ellison, Jesse, 112–116
Emotional neglect, 108–109

F

A Fable (Faulkner), 37
Falkner, Dean, 17, 24, 39–40
Falkner, John (brother), 17, 38
Falkner, John (grandfather), 33–34
Falkner, Maud Butler, 35–39
Falkner, Murry (father), 34–40
Falkner, Murry (Jack) (brother), 17, 37–38
Family dysfunction
    causes of, 9
    child neglect and, 107–111
    in Faulkner's family, 33–40
    in *As I Lay Dying*, 10, 49–54
    results of, 9–10
    signs of, 11
    stories of, 9
Fathers/fatherhood, 123–128, *126*
Faulkner, Alabama, 24
Faulkner, Estelle, 24, *85*
Faulkner, Jill, 24, 28
Faulkner, William
    on the Bundren family, 42–48
    dysfunctional family of, 33–40
    early life of, 17–18, 37–40
    economic struggles of, 26–32
    family responsibilities of, 23–24
    influences on, 17–18
    literary reputation of, 24–25
    marriage of, 19, 24
    in military, 18–19
    personal problems of, 24
    photo of, *22, 29, 46, 85*
    short stories of, 30–32
    stylistic innovations of, 20
    themes in, 17
    writing career of, 16–25
Favoritism, parental, 40, 129–135
Feinberg, Mark, 132–133
Female action, 73–74
Female characters, 23, 65–70
Female sexuality, 65–69, 81–83, 86–87
Feminine principle, 72–73, 78
Femininity, 82–83
Fish, as symbol, 70, 103, 105
Fisher, Helen, 113
Fleming, Alison, 120
Fowler, Doreen, 87
Franklin, Cornell, 18, 19
Fraternal conflict, 60–61

G

Gambling, 119
Gender, attitudes toward, 62–65
Go Down, Moses (Faulkner), 24

H

Heat stroke, 91–92
Hewson, Marc, 71–80
Hobson, Fred, 62
Horn, Wade, 127
Horse, as symbol, 42–43, 52–53, 59, 78, 84
Housework, 114
Howe, Irving, 88, 102

I

Intruder in the Dust (Faulkner), 24, 25
Isay, Jane, 130

J

Jayson, Sharon, 129–135
Jenkins, Jennifer, 134
Jewel (*As I Lay Dying*)
    Addie and, 66, 77–78, 84
    as alien, 42–43
    Cash and, 60
    character of, 21, 56, 95–100
    Darl and, 98–99
    horse of, 52–54, 59, 78, 84, 99
    impulsiveness of, 97–98
    as man of action, 96–97, 99–100
    physical description of, 95–96, 97
    rebellion by, 59
    swearing by, 96–97, 98
    woodenness of, 95–96

K

Kennedy, Laurel, 130
Kincaid, Nanci, 62–70
King, Roma, Jr., 102

Kinsley, Craig, 119–121
Kirk, Robert, 89
Kramer, Laurie, 131, 133, 134

L

Lafe (*As I Lay Dying*), 54, 67
Lewis, Sinclair, 31
Libby, Ellen Weber, 134–135
Life, 74
Love, 66, 77–78, 115–116

M

Madness, 45–47, 50–51
Male characters, 23
Male inaction, 73–74
Male-female relationships, 65–67
The Mansion (Faulkner), 25
Marital relationships, 65–66
Marriage, 112–116, 125, 127
Masculinity, 72–73, 82
Maternal neurons, 119–121
May, Josie, 30
McHale, Susan, 133
McKenna, Maggie, 107–111
Meaninglessness, 51–52
Mencken, H.L., 31
Mohler, Henry K., 91
Monogamy, 113
Mosely (*As I Lay Dying*), 51
Mother-child relationships, 52–53, 56, 59–61, 71–80, 83–87, 129–135
Mother-father relationship, 124–125
Motherhood, 47–48, 75–76, 81–84, 86–87, 117–122

Index

A Mountain Victory (Faulkner), 30–31
Mules, symbolism of, 65, *77*

N

National Alliance of Children's Trust and Prevention Funds, 107
Nielson, Paul, 84
Nietzsche, Friedrich, 63
Nobel Prize, 25
Nuclear family, 113

O

O'Connor, Cailin, 107–111
Oedipus, 9
Oldham, Estelle, 17, 18, 19
O'Shea, Brenda, 133

P

Parents
    fathers, 123–128
    favoritism by, 40, 129–135
    neglectful, 107–111
    relationship between, 124–125
    See also Mother-child relationships
Parker-Pope, Tara, 115–116
Patriarchy, 74–75, 87
Patterson, Rusty, 28
Plumez, Jacqueline, 130, 131
Popenoe, David, 123–124
The Portable Faulkner (Cowley), 25
Poverty, 10, 11, 110–111
Psychosocial development, 127–128

R

Race, 10
Red Leaves (Faukner), 30
The Reivers (Faulkner), 25, 37
Religious suppression, 62–70
Rippetoe, Rita, 88–94
Romaine, Paul, 31
Rosenberg, Jeffrey, 123–128
Rossky, William, 49–54
Rubin, Gayle, 65

S

Sanctuary (Faulkner), 19
Sexuality
    attitudes toward, 62–65
    female, 65–69, 81–83, 86–87
Shegog, Robert R., 26
Shegog house, 24, 26–29
Sibling relationships
    in Faulkner's family, 38, 39–40
    in *As I Lay Dying*, 45–47, 57–58, 60–61, 98–99
    parental favoritism and, 129–135
Sin, 84
Smith, Harrison, 19
Sojourner, Mary, 117–122
The Sound and the Fury (Faulkner), 19, 20, 23
South
    poverty in, 10
    religious suppression in, 62–70
Steinem, Gloria, 114
Stone, Phil, 17–18
Swain, James, 120
Swearing, 97, 98
Symbolism
    of cows, 64–65, 67, *68*

of fish, 70, 103, 105
of horse, 42–43, 52–53, 59, 78, 84
of mules, 65, *77*
of Vardaman, 102

T

That Evening Sun Go Down (Faulkner), 31
Toothlessness, 70, 89, 92, *93*, 94
The Town (Faulkner), 25
Turner, William, 26

V

Vardaman (*As I Lay Dying*)
    Addie and, 53
    character of, 21, 54
    coping by, 50, 51
    grief of, 76–77, 104–105
    as idiot, 101–102, 105
    reaction to death by, 101–105
    revenge of, 58
    state of mind of, 44–45
    as symbol, 102
    as young child, 102–103

Vernon Tull (*As I Lay Dying*), 51, 52, 56, 90
Villain, 45

W

Wagner-Martin, Linda, 16–25
Wasson, Ben, 18, 28
Watkins, Floyd C., 101–105
Wilcox, W. Bradford, 123–128
Wilkins, Sallie Murry, 17
Wilson, Sue, 135
Wittenberg, Judith Bryant, 33–40
Women
    characters, 23, 65–70
    Faulkner's fear of, 70
    instinct for mothering and, 117–122
    as shelter and food, 69–70
    status of, 113–114
    suppression of, 65–70
    in workforce, 114–115
Wood, Amy Louise, 81–87
World War I, 10, 18

Y

Young, Stark, 18

www.ingramcontent.com/pod-product-compliance
Lightning Source LLC
Chambersburg PA
CBHW072047290426
44110CB00014B/1581